The typographic scene

WALTER TRACY

The typographic scene

Gordon Fraser · London

First published 1988 by
Gordon Fraser Gallery Ltd London and Bedford

BRITISH LIBRARY CATALOGUING IN PUBLICATION DATA

Tracy, Walter
    The Typographic Scene
    1. Typography. Design, 1900–1980
    I. Title
    686.2'2

ISBN 0 86092 112 3

Typeset in Monophoto Sabon by August Filmsetting,
Haydock, St. Helens
Printed by the Alden Press, Oxford
Bound by Hunter and Foulis, Edinburgh

Contents

Preface and acknowledgements

Like other designers, typographers need to have an attitude to their subject – a point of view and a set of standards by which to judge the type designs they are offered and the way people use them. Knowledge of the facts of the subject does not by itself automatically produce wisdom; it needs to be distilled and matured. Experience usually does that, and the opinions of others may accelerate the process.

It is just sixty years since I first took up a composing stick and began to look at type and the way it was used, so my views of twentieth-century typography have a long perspective. With time for reflection, it has seemed to me that about some aspects of the subject and some people connected with it a degree of mythologising has occurred, and I have chosen to be critical of ideas and attitudes where I judge them to be unsound. Hence these essays, which are offered in the hope that they will help those interested in typographic design to make an objective appraisal of it. I hope, though, that the reader will not accept my opinions without question, but will simply take them for what they are worth.

I am glad to express my gratitude to James Mosley, who has frequently suggested new lines of thought; to the always helpful staff of the St Bride Printing Library; to Rose Tracy, for help with *archy*; and to Peter Guy, who encouraged me to postpone idleness a little longer.

                                                             W.T.

Introduction

The last decade of the nineteenth century has been called, by more than one writer, the period of the 'Revival of Printing'. That was the title of a chapter in Holbrook Jackson's *The Eighteen Nineties* (1913), in which he surveyed the work of the Kelmscott, Vale, Eragny and Doves presses, those remarkable endeavours which were conducted by idealists whose view of the book as an object of art and craft was far removed from the one held by the commercial publisher and the ordinary reader. 'Printing' – as in the title of Stanley Morison's *Four Centuries of Fine Printing* – has often been interpreted as '*book* printing', but Holbrook Jackson had shown elsewhere in *The Eighteen Nineties* that in that short period there was a great deal more activity in printing than was represented in the work of the private presses and the book publisher. He remarked that no other decade in English history had produced so many distinctive and ambitious publications; he listed nearly a score of periodicals devoted to literature and the arts, at various levels of taste and popular appeal. He was discussing affairs in Britain, or he might have noted that in the very month in 1894 that John Lane introduced *The Yellow Book* in London, the first number of *The Chap-Book* was issued in Cambridge, Massachusetts, by Herbert Stuart Stone and Hannibal Ingalls Kimball.

In those last years of the century there were many artists and designers engaged in decorating the covers and bindings of magazines and books, producing lettering for the advertisements put out by the expanding department stores, and even occasionally instructing a printer in the sort of type to be used in a particular piece of printing. But the person who did that as a full-time occupation, the professional typographer, was yet to come. He is a figure of the twentieth century. Indeed, it was not until a quarter of this present century had come and gone that the work of typographers and the type faces that were created for their use began to be seen as a distinctive aspect of publishing, printing and advertising.

The development of the typographic scene, with the changes that have occurred in the course of it, is outlined in the first three essays in this book. It is intended as a background for two particular aspects of the scene: the argument for and against symmetrical and asymmetrical arrangement; and the reforms that have been proposed from time to time.

The common element in all typographic work is the word. Not everyone has been content with its form, or with the letters of which it is composed. The desire to rectify the English language – its spelling, that is, not its grammar – began to be expressed long ago, and it has had its supporters during the present century. Some reformers have also been dissatisfied with the alphabets we use and have urged that two is one too many, or have thought them inadequate and that new characters should be added, in the cause of efficiency if not of typographic elegance. A later essay here considers such notions, and offers a personal opinion of the value of them, on the premise that the basic elements in typography, the letter and the word, are the consequences of human invention and convention, the natural outcome of trend and consensus, and are as effective (and as illogical) as are people themselves.

Advent

To publishers and others concerned with presenting words in visible form to the public, in print or on a screen, 'typography' means the process of making the words visually attractive and effective; and a typographer is a person professionally trained to perform that task, and earns a living by doing so. The definition excludes artists like James McNeill Whistler, whose inventive designing of the books he wrote is an interesting aspect of his artistic awareness but does not entitle him to be called a typographer. Nor does that definition of 'typography' admit concrete or mimetic poetry, or those abstract assemblages of geometric forms and letters devised by some artists of the 1920s, which, however stimulating they may have been to an observer like Jan Tschichold, had their genesis in an internal impulse in the artist and not in a commission from an external source. Typography is a professional activity directed towards a practical, and usually commercial, result.

The professional typographer hardly existed before the beginning of the twentieth century; but the terms 'typography' and 'typographer' have a long history. Joseph Moxon, whose *Mechanick Exercises on the Whole Art of Printing*, the earliest manual on the subject, was published in 1683–4, thought the typographer should be not just a printer but a person well versed in all the activities connected with printing, from punch-cutting to ink making. Fournier, in the introduction to his *Manuel Typographique* (1764), took the same view; he referred to the three indispensable parts of typography – punch-cutting, type founding and printing – and said that only someone who had knowledge of all three could properly be called a typographer. At that time, there *were* such people: Fournier himself, and then Francois-Ambroise Didot and his sons Pierre and Firmin; but they were not typical, and to postulate a person of comprehensive technical knowledge and experience, to be awarded the title of 'typographer' as a mark of acclaim, was rhetorical rather than realistic; type founding and printing having long ago become quite separate crafts, each of them with its own grand masters.

The word 'typography' was then being used simply as a rather high-flown synonym for printing (and is still sometimes so used: see, for instance, Marshall McLuhan's *The Gutenberg Galaxy*). It took on a more precise and justifiable meaning, though still a technical one, during the nineteenth century, when it came to mean relief or letterpress printing as distinct from the intaglio and lithographic processes. (Hence the adjective in the somewhat odd title of Legros and Grant's well-known *Typographical Print-ing Surfaces*, 1916.) What was absent, though, was any sugges-tion that the term included *design* as well as technique; design, that is, as a matter of taste, choice and arrangement. Not until the 1890s did aesthetic principles begin to be applied to printed work in a clearly visible way, though the need for them had been felt for some time before that. In 1882 Henry Stevens of Vermont, then living in Britain, had expressed a critical view of the debased quality of book work. He asked, 'Who spoils our new English books?'[1] and accused everybody in sight: the author, publisher, printer, reader, compositor, pressman, paper-maker, ink-maker, book-binder and, not least, the customer – all of them sinners by omission or commission. He thought there was a painful lack of harmony apparent in what was produced, and he said he would like to see a school of typography established in England, so that everyone concerned could study and practise the 'laws of propor-tion, taste and workmanship' that had been so well observed in the past. He spoke with regret of the decline in the standard of printing during the forty years since the fine work done by Charles Whittingham at his Chiswick Press for the publisher William Pickering.

The Caslon type which Whittingham had revived in 1844 had fallen into disuse. Arthur Turnure (one of the founders of the Grolier Club of New York in 1884) revived the type for the first issue of *Vogue* magazine in the autumn of 1892.[2] It was one of the three body types with which Updike started his Merrymount Press in Boston in 1893.[3] Two years later Will Bradley discovered it for himself and used it in his short-lived Wayside Press at Springfield, Mass.;[4] and there were others who, disliking the chilly 'modern' faces so prevalent at the time, adopted the type as a welcome change. This second revival of Caslon is visible evidence of individual efforts to improve the state of printing. It occurred in Britain, too. Caslon was used in many of the publi-cations issued by Elkin Matthews and John Lane: *The Yellow Book*, for example, and, in conjunction with a modernised old style, in Oscar Wilde's *The Sphinx*, which was designed by Charles Ricketts, an important figure in the 'aesthetic move-ment'.[5] The book was a key item in that movement, its design perfectly expressing Wilde's exotic text. It impressed Bruce Rogers but it is a little odd that he should have said, as late as 1939, 'I know of no lovelier, entirely modern, book.'[6] The *Yellow Book* and other publications from London were distributed in Chicago by Way & Williams and in Boston by Copeland & Day and were much admired for their refreshing inventiveness. A very different but even more potent source of interest was the work of the private press movement in England, and particularly William Morris's Kelmscott Press. Its creations, with their opulence of illustration, were remarkable feats of craftsmanship and in

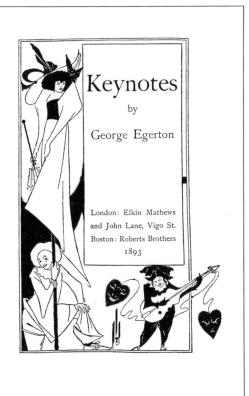

Keynotes

by

George Egerton

London: Elkin Mathews
and John Lane, Vigo St.
Boston: Roberts Brothers
1893

For what was it else within me wrought
But, I fear, the new strong wine of love
That made my tongue so stammer and trip
When I saw the treasured splendour, her hand,
Come sliding out of her sacred glove,
And the sunlight broke from her lip?

10.

I have play'd with her when a child;
She remembers it now we meet.
Ah well, well, well, I may be beguiled
By some coquettish deceit.
Yet, if she were not a cheat,
If Maud were all that she seem'd,
And her smile had all that I dream'd,
Then the world were not so bitter
But a smile could make it sweet.

VII.

ID I hear it half in a doze
Long since, I know not where?
Did I dream it an hour ago,
When asleep in this arm-chair?

2.

Men were drinking together,
Drinking and talking of me;
20

THE SPHINX BY OSCAR WILDE

WITH DECORATIONS BY CHARLES RICKETTS
LONDON MDCCCXCIV
ELKIN MATHEWS AND JOHN LANE. AT THE SIGN OF THE BODLEY HEAD.

Title page of one of the
Keynotes series published by
John Lane; decorated by
Aubrey Beardsley

A page in William Morris's
Golden type

Title page of *The Sphinx*
(1894); title in black,
decoration in brown,
subscript in green

overwhelming contrast to the characterless work of even the most respected commercial printers of the time.

The effect of all this was revelatory and stimulating, and the sense of dissatisfaction at the dismal state of the general run of print was replaced by a positive desire to show what should and could be done to make printed things elegant and pleasurable. By the turn of the century in the United States 'typography' was taking on a specific meaning: the discriminating choice of paper, colour, type and decoration, and the harmonious assembling of them into an effective whole. And it was becoming evident that the work was of a professional order, to be done by a specialist, a 'typographer', associated with, but not necessarily a member of, the printing house.

Bruce Rogers was one of the first of them. After a couple of books showing the influence of Kelmscott he set his own course, and became in time one of the most distinguished book designers of the twentieth century. Another designer who was in at the beginning was Will Bradley, who made his mark in a different area of printing. In his role as illustrator, during the last years of the nineties, he sedulously imitated the manner of Burne-Jones's illustrations for Kelmscott and also the very individual style of Beardsley's work, sometimes combining them in the same design.[7] When he undertook a campaign of typographic publicity for American Type Founders[8] and then became design editor for *Collier's* and other magazines he displayed another talent: considerable ability in the attractive use of type. No doubt his work had a beneficial influence on competitive journals and the advertisements that appeared in them.

The revival of old style types, and the faces derived from fifteenth-century romans specially created for some of the English private presses, produced a desire for knowledge of typographic history. De Vinne's *Historic Printing Types*, an enlargement of a lecture he gave to the Grolier Club, must have been welcomed when it was published in 1886. One of the first of those who taught the subject was D. B. Updike, the eminent Boston printer. From 1911 to 1916 he lectured at Harvard on type designs from the middle of the fifteenth century through to the Caslon revival. The text of his talks, revised and amplified, was published in 1922, under the title *Printing Types, their History, Form and Use*. It was immediately perceived as essential reading for any aspiring typographer.

In the United States, then, typography, the *designing* of print, was a recognised and developing profession by the end of the first decade of this century; a fact demonstrated by the establishing in 1914 of the American Institute of Graphic Arts as a centre for the promotion of interest in good design. In Britain things began rather more slowly. The Kelmscott work was treated with awed respect by scholars and collectors but had little effect on the

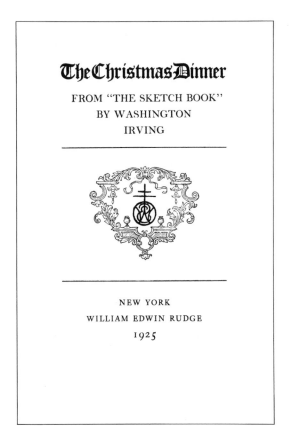

A title page by Bruce Rogers, 1925; and one from the ATF *American Chap-Book*, April 1905; designed by Will Bradley, using Frederic Goudy's Pabst Old Style

general printer. The work of Charles Ricketts and the books produced by John Lane's Bodley Head were an acquired taste; admired by some, scorned by others, with much hostility for anything and anyone connected with Wilde. The few signs of typographic endeavour, like the engaging of Herbert Horne by Chatto and Windus and The Medici Society to design types for their own use, were too isolated to have much influence. The supplement on printing issued by *The Times* in September 1912 had only one vague reference to a typographer (and that from an American correspondent). However, the term was clearly used in the modern sense just a few months later, in *The Imprint*. That journal, which began in January 1913 and ceased after nine numbers, was an attempt by Gerard Meynell and others to arouse interest in good printing. An editorial note in the first issue referred to the poor appearance of current work, and went on: 'It is refreshing, however, to find one of the most prominent businessmen willing to avail himself of the knowledge and trained taste of the typographer.' (Gordon Selfridge, the American owner of the famous Oxford Street department store, was offering a prize of ten guineas in a letter-heading competition.) *The Imprint* was the cause of an event that turned out to be of great significance. In its first number there was an offer of a place in its office for a young man of good education and preferably with some experience in publishing and advertising. A dissatisfied bank clerk named Stanley Morison, of modest education and no experience, applied for the post, impressed Gerard Meynell and was taken on. When *The Imprint* ceased in November 1913 Morison moved to the publishing house where Francis Meynell was in charge of production. He had taken the first steps in a life of typographic study and practice that was to make him, in the opinion of many, the most eminent scholar in the history of typography.

Looking back to that period Meynell described it as 'a dreary typographic epoch ... The function of typographer was non-existent; the printer's foreman compositor was left to do the designing.'[9] That was not quite the case. Joseph Thorp practised as a designer of printing, and his *Printing for Business* (1918) was one of the first attempts to extend typographic designing from the book to the commercial field. But not until the 1914–18 war ended did British typography begin to flourish in anything like a substantial way.

At the end of the next decade, during which *The Fleuron* had considerable influence in promoting the cause of good typography, Stanley Morison was able, in the postscript to the final volume, to refer to the increase in typographical material and activity he had observed during his five years as editor. 'New types were being cut; new presses being established; printing became "fine" printing; and printers, publishers and booksellers, between them, made typography fashionable.' It was not, of course, the book world alone that was making typography interesting. It would be more precise to say that while the book publishers were assuming the responsibility for the appearance of their books instead of leaving it to the printer, and were recognising that design needs serious study and effort, the publicity typographers, activated by the need to make their work attractive as well as readable, were taking advantage of the new display types that were coming forward and were themselves becoming increasingly important figures on the typographic scene.

HAROLD CURWEN OF T[
CURWEN PRES[
has studied under one of the editors of [
Magazine, as well as under other leader[
the movement for improving the style[
commercial printing.

THE STAFF OF TH[
CURWEN PRES[
has been trained so that it is able, with
present-day materials, to produce the
results in artistic and forceful Catalog[
Show Cards, Pamphlets, Labels, etc.,
also in the printing and binding of beaut[
books of every description.

Mr. Curwen requests permission to call
your address, or to send examples of
work executed at

THE CURWEN PRESS,
Plaistow, London, E.
'Phone: EAST 1737 (3 lines).

An early sign of the intention[
a printing house that became
famous for the quality of its
typography: advertisement in
The Imprint, January 1913

The march of type

The revival of the Caslon type and the introduction of Scotch roman on both sides of the Atlantic cannot have satisfied typographers for very long; but any attempts they made to persuade type founders and printers that additions to the repertoire were not only desirable but necessary were slow to take effect. The founders' response, such as it was, took two forms: the introduction of a few newly created designs, and the reviving of type faces of the past. A summary of the development of type design from the beginning of this century up to about 1970 will be helpful in appreciating the nature of the changes that have occurred during the period.

One of the earliest new faces to appear, the Century type, is of continuing interest, at least in Britain. The first version of it was a strengthened 'modern' face, created for the text of the *Century* magazine, in which it first appeared in 1895. T. L. De Vinne, whose printing office produced the magazine, wrote that the new type was 'modelled and cut' by Linn Boyd Benton of American Type Founders. 'To proportion the type for a large page in two columns and with narrow margins, and to give the usual amount of text in the *Century* page, the characters were compressed a trifle.'[1] In fact, the face was quite noticeably condensed, and narrower than the standard faces on which the compositors' scale of piece-work was based. (Composition of type by hand had not yet been superseded by the composing machine.)[2] To conform to the union standard American Type Founders produced for the general trade a wider version of the Century face; that is, a version of normal proportions of width to height, and to distinguish the face from the first version they called it Century 'Expanded'. The makers of the Linotype and Ludlow machines soon adopted the design *and* the name, and others have followed the same course. The term 'Expanded' must have puzzled many people*, the type being in no way abnormal, but American suppliers continue to use it. Linotype in Britain discarded the term in its 1953 specimen book, where the type is shown as Century, *tout court*. Century Bold, created by Morris Fuller Benton and one of the earliest 'related' bold faces, came a little later. Its unusual though perfectly acceptable feature is the absence of a serif on the inner side of the right leg of the letters n and m. The great merit of the design is that though it is visibly more emphatic than the Century roman the thickness of the strokes and the

---

* Another example of this kind of confusing nomenclature is Monotype's Modern Extended No. 7, familiar to British printers. It is actually a normal-width version of their Series 1, which was a copy of a slightly condensed news text type made by Miller and Richard of Edinburgh in the 1890s.

width of the whites in enclosed characters such as o, p and e are well balanced. The face has always been popular for headline use in the British press; *The Independent*, the 'quality' daily newspaper which was introduced in Britain in October 1986, uses Century roman and bold for all its headings, to good effect.

A touch of tear gas with the *moules feuilletées*

US actors keep bar on *Phantom* star

Century and Century Bold in *The Independent*, 24 June 198 (reduced). Note the difference the style of the italics

Another new face to appear about the same time as Century was the one designed in 1900 by the architect Bertram Goodhue for the Cheltenham Press of New York, and issued in a range of sizes and variations during the next few years by ATF and Mergenthaler Linotype. In his *Printing Types*[3] Updike was surprisingly kind about the Cheltenham face – perhaps out of regard for Goodhue, who had drawn the Merrymount type for him. The Cheltenham design owed little or nothing to any previous style. Its lack of character and elegance ought to have repelled more people than it did (the same is true today); and its chief (some would say 'only') merit was that it printed well, having no thin strokes or fragile elements. Its novelty would have accounted for its early favour; but in fact the popularity of the Cheltenham family continued all over the world for more than thirty years, a phenomenon in the history of type design.

Equally ubiquitous was the Bodoni face introduced by ATF in 1911, imitated by Linotype in 1914, and shortly by everyone else. The fact that the design was a synthetic, not a true, version of Bodoni's types was of more interest to the specialist than to the majority of typographers and printers, who welcomed it as an alternative to the over-familiar old style faces then available. The Cloister type issued by ATF in 1914 also received warm approval, especially as the founders were able to say that the roman was a close version of the fifteenth-century Jenson type that had been so much admired by William Morris.

The first creative effort by the American Linotype company was also an earnest revival of an early roman. It appeared in 1915 and was called Benedictine; a dull design, loosely fitted and distinctly heavy. Its companion italic, adapted from the roman, was a compound of awkward letter forms. A lighter version was issued a few years later, with only moderate success. Much more

Bodoni   *Bodoni Italic*
Bodoni Bold
Bodoni Bold Italic

AFT Bodoni, and Cloister, both by Morris Fuller Benton, adapted from early models

Cloister Oldstyle
Cloister Italic

Cloister Bold
Cloister Bold Italic

℃ This Calendar Book is based upon that used by Benedictis, also called Plato

Benedictine, adapted by Joseph E. Hill, 1915

KEEP SILENCE, AND *A TIME TO SPEAK;* A time to love, and a time to hate ; a time of *war, and a time of peace.* What *profit hath he that*

Kennerley, designed by Frederic Goudy; the roman 1911, the italic 1918

Goudy Old Style *and Italic*

Goudy Oldstyle, 1915, ATF

EXQUISITE for clearness

Fry's Baskerville perhaps cut by Isaac Moore, c.1758

to the approval of the advertising typographer were two faces by Frederic Goudy: his Kennerley, the roman of which was first seen in 1911 and the italic some years later, the design then being acquired by Lanston Monotype in 1920; and his Goudy Oldstyle (1915), a fine design that has deserved its continuing popularity. In 1917 ATF introduced the Baskerville roman they had obtained from the Stephenson Blake foundry in England. It was actually the type known as Fry's Baskerville, which some think is superior to the original. McMurtrie, writing in 1924, said the face had received far too little attention.[4] (Baskerville's day had yet to come.) Much more interesting at the time were the versions of Garamond appearing on the scene: the A T F face in 1919 and Lanston Monotype's Garamont (from letter drawings by Goudy) in 1922.

McMurtrie's short survey was his selection of the best of the

THIS FINE AND CLASSICAL FACE, Drawn By Frederic W. Goudy For The Monotype in 1923, was based upon a type

Garamont, after Jannon's type, c.1615. Lanston Monotype, 1922

ARTISTIC TASTE
For Selection of Type

Plantin Old Style, so called by the P. M. Shanks foundry, London, c. 1907. Identical with New Caslon, Inland Type Foundry, St. Louis, 1905

ℚ Westminster Old Style
suits all Classes of Work

Westminster (Della Robbia, by T. M. Cleland, Lanston Monotype, 1903)

BRITISH Museum

Chippendale (Artcraft, by Robert Wiebking, Barnhart Bros. and Spindler, 1912)

types introduced in America in the first twenty years of this century. His list had a few good faces in it, but it was not an impressive collection. In Britain things were little better. The type founders had introduced the plain but undistinguished Windsor and Chatsworth and, from America, the strengthened version of Caslon that was renamed, confusingly, Plantin Old Style, and they had imported the Della Robbia and Artcraft faces, issued as Westminster and Chippendale. Those were all display faces, and they became popular in jobbing work. The Linotype company concentrated on supplying the needs of the newspaper printers of Britain and Europe, which meant imitating for the machine the foundry types the newspapers had been using for most of the nineteenth century. Monotype, too, spent their early years in reproducing existing type faces. Their first hundred faces were an accumulation of latins, antiques, moderns and other familiar types of the period, with Gloucester, a version of Cheltenham, making a late appearance as Series 99. But Series 101 was a very different matter: the excellent Imprint Old Face, which was seen in the first number of *The Imprint* in January 1913. To say that the face was a regulated version of Caslon is not enough; it was a genuine creative effort by the Monotype drawing office. Later

Imprint
fgrhRM*fgkyw*

Imprint Old Face, Monotype UK, 1912

Plantin 110
kfgrhjRM*fgkyw*

Plantin Series 110, Monotype UK, 1913

Poliphilus 170, abf
Blado 119 fgky

Poliphilus, cut by Griffo, Bologna, 1499; Monotype, 192

Fournier 185
fghjRM*fgkyw*

Fournier, by P. S. Fournier, Paris, 1742; Monotype, 1925

Bembo 270
fgrhjRM*fgkyw*

Bembo, by Griffo, Bologna, 14 Monotype, 1929

that year Monotype introduced the Plantin Series 110, which was derived from a sixteenth-century old-style type. Though somewhat over-regulated it has become a twentieth-century classic.

If it had not been for the war of 1914–18 the expansion of typographic activity in Britain might have occurred sooner. As it was, not until the mid-twenties did the creative impulse in type design and in typography itself really begin to flourish. The fifteen years up to the beginning of the second world war formed a period of remarkable development in type design, much of it created or instigated by people outside the source of manufacture. To record all the many faces produced in the period (most of them still available) would throw this present account out of balance. A selection will suffice to indicate the nature of the inventiveness of the period; and it will clarify the course of events to deal with the faces according to the role for which they were created: first, the text types, meant for passages of continuous reading, and then the display types, plain or decorative, intended for headings in advertisements or magazine features.

For obvious reasons it was the composing machine manufacturers whose chief interest was in text types. It should not be invidious to start with the British developments, since in historical terms it was the Monotype company in England which made the first notable efforts. Whether or not there was a 'programme', a pre-conceived list of types to be produced, as Stanley Morison, their typographical adviser, claimed, or simply his general sense of the need for development – to be particularised as and when suitable subjects were revealed by research – is a matter for the historian or biographer. The working typographer is interested in what was actually done.

Monotype's Garamond and Baskerville had been issued in 1923, and then, under Morison's scholarly guidance, there followed during the next few years a number of fine revivals: Poliphilus, Fournier, Bembo, Bell, Walbaum and Van Dijck. Some designs were acquired: Lutetia and Romulus from a Dutch source, and Centaur, Goudy Modern and Emerson from America. Those were all book types, seriously conceived and well executed, though not equally successful in the commercial sense. Monotype's admirable Ehrhardt appeared in 1938. It began as a version of the so-called Janson type which Mergenthaler Linotype had reproduced with acclaim in America; but Monotype re-modelled the design to such an extent that the face is as different from Janson as Imprint is from Caslon. Two text faces by Eric Gill were commissioned by Monotype in the same period: Perpetua, which as a text type has been esteemed more than it has been used; and Solus, a sort of Perpetua with Bodoni-style serifs, rightly disregarded by the typographer and printer. And, still on the subject of text types, the one that was created by

Bell, *Ser. 341*
kkfgrhjRM*fgkyw*

Bell: cut by Richard Austin, 1788: Monotype, 1930

Walbaum
fgrhjRM*fgkyw*

Walbaum, by J.E. Walbaum, Weimar c. 1803; Monotype, 1930

Van *Dijck* Ser. 203
fgrhjRM*fgkyw*

Van Dijck, by C. van Dijck, Amsterdam, c.1660; Monotype, 1937–8

Lutetia 255
fgrhjRM*fgkyw*

Lutetia, designed by Jan van Krimpen, Haarlem, 1925; Monotype, 1928

Romulus 458
fgrhjRM*fghyw*

Romulus, by J. van Krimpen, Enschedé and Monotype, 1931–9

Centaur 252
fgehaRM*fgkqw*

Centaur, designed by Bruce Rogers, 1914, after Jenson, 1470; Monotype, 1929

Goudy M^{ODERN} 249
fgrhjRM*fgkyw*

Goudy Modern, by F. W. Goudy, 1918; Monotype, 1928

Morison for a newspaper – the Times Roman introduced in 1932 – has for the past half-century been so omnipresent as to seem positively immortal.

The text faces introduced by Monotype in those inter-war years had a remarkably stimulating effect on British typography,

English Politicals

Janson, by Nicolas Kis, Amsterdam, 1685

Perpetua 239
afgrhjRMfgkyw

Perpetua, designed by Eric Gill for Monotype, 1929

SOLUS an Eric Gill design

Solus, by Eric Gill, Monotype, 1929

but less so in the United States, where the dominant source of supply was Mergenthaler Linotype. However, the American scene gained great advantage from the type faces instigated by George W. Jones, the eminent English printer, for the British Linotype company. The most important was the Granjon face issued in 1924 and acknowledged by Beatrice Warde of Monotype to be a true Garamond,[5] distinguished in design, smoothly legible, and without distracting features – though she could not resist a mildly sarcastic reference to the non-kerning f. (A rejoinder about the problems caused in single type composition by such words as offhand, aufbessern and Kafka would probably have looked undignified!) Granjon was immediately acquired by Mergenthaler Linotype. It became one of the most admired of book types; Bruce Rogers used it many times to excel-

The Grolier Club, New York

LE MIROIR DE L'AME.
from an unsigned edition

lent effect. The Estienne face was another revival of a sixteenth-century old style organised by Jones that found favour for a time in America. And there was the Baskerville. In 1920 Bruce Rogers had persuaded the University Press at Harvard to obtain a font of type cast from matrices struck from the original Baskerville punches which Rogers had discovered to be in Paris.[6] No doubt

Emerson 320
fgrhjRMfgkyw

Emerson, by Joseph Blument
1931; Monotype, 1936

Ehrhardt 45:
fgrhjRMfgkyw

Ehrhardt, adapted by Monoty
1937 from a face cut by Nicol
Amsterdam, 1685

Times New Rom. 3: and Wide 4:
efgrhjRMfgkyw
efgrhjRMfgkyw

Times Roman, by Stanley Mc
for *The Times*, 1932; made by
Monotype and Linotype and
issued to the general trade 19

Granjon, by Claude
Garamond, c.1550;
Linotype UK, 1924

Estienne, a Garamond face?;
Linotype UK, 1930

the Linotype office in New York knew of this, and they must certainly have known of McMurtrie's recommendation of the ATF version[7] and of the Baskerville made by Monotype in Britain. Mergenthaler asked George W. Jones to obtain a supply of the foundry type from Paris, to supervise the production of letter drawings at the Linotype plant in north-west England, and to supply copies of them to the New York plant for the making of patterns, punches and matrices. The outcome was a Baskerville remarkably close to the original. I have always thought it rather dull, and much prefer another type which Jones revived in 1934 – the face he named Georgian, derived from a late eighteenth-century type made in Scotland after the Baskerville model but with more colour and character. It can be seen in Trollope's *The Warden* in the paperback World's Classics series, and in the Penguin American Library edition of Hawthorne's *Scarlet Letter*.

Towards the end of the inter-war period Mergenthaler Linotype issued three original text types: Electra (1935), a fine book type; Caledonia (1938), almost as distinguished and rather more versatile because its bold version was extended to display sizes; and, in the following year, Fairfield, a book face of particular charm. The company had earlier been active in developing a number of text faces for a quite different but equally important area of printing: the newspaper field, an area in which the Monotype system, with its keyboarding and casting as separate

TEN MINUTES' ADVICE
by John Archdeacon, Printer

Georgian, possibly cut by Alexander Wilson, Glasgow c.1760; Linotype UK, 1934

THE QUICK brown fox jumps over the lazy dog. How is one to assess and evaluate a type face in terms of its esthetic design. Why do the pace-makers in the art *The quick brown fox jumps over the* *The quick brown fox jumps over the*

Electra, designed by W. A. Dwiggins; Linotype US, 1935

THE QUICK brown fox jumps over the lazy dog. How is one to assess and evaluate a type face in terms of its esthetic design. Why do the pace-makers in the *art of printing rave over a specific face of type? What do they see in it? Why is*

Caledonia, by W. A. Dwiggins; Linotype US, 1938

The General History of Quadrupeds was published in 1790. Encouraged by the astonishing success of his venture, Bewick went on with the subject nearest his heart, the *History of British Birds*. After

Fairfield, designed by Rudolph Ruzicka: Linotype US, 1939

functions, had no place. Linotype's first and most significant news face was Ionic, issued in 1926. It was not, as Stanley Morison thought,[8] simply a re-cutting of the type of that name first produced in the middle of the nineteenth century, but the final one of a number of different versions of it; a painstaking effort to develop a news text type suitable for the mass-production techniques of the time. It was immediately successful; several of Britain's leading newspapers still use it. Because different papers had particular production requirements, or simply needed to distinguish themselves from a competitor, Linotype produced several variations of Ionic during the next few years: Textype, Excelsior (still very popular in the European press), Opticon and Paragon – all soon to be superseded in most American newspapers by Linotype's Corona face, which was

Millions of words, in thousands of newspapers and magazines, are printed and read daily. All over the world news is necessary to the everyday routine of many millions of people. The public appetite for news is enormous, and the man who never reads a newspaper is news himself.

Ionic, Linotype US, 1926

Millions of words, in thousands of newspapers and magazines, are printed and read daily. All over the world news is necessary to the everyday routine of many millions of people. The public appetite for news is enormous, and the man who never reads a newspaper is news himself.

Excelsior, Linotype US, 1931

Millions of words, in thou of newspapers and maga are printed and read daily over the world news is nece to the everyday routine of millions of people. The p appetite for news is enor and the man who never re newspaper is news himself

Corona, Linotype US, 1941

introduced in 1941. Considering the essential role of the newspaper in the lives of millions, the creation of type faces for newspapers is as important in its own way as the designing of types for books. The fact that stylishness or 'character' in news types would be out of place and even detrimental does not diminish their significance.

In the twenties and thirties, then, when the mechanical composing machines had become thoroughly established, it was the manufacturers who dominated the development of text types. The results were largely a matter of revivals and adaptations, with comparatively little in the way of contemporary work. With regard to *display* types the reverse was the case. The type foundries had lost their trade in text types to the composing machines, so to maintain their existence they were obliged to concentrate their energies on the production of faces that would gain the favour of the typographer in the rapidly expanding field of advertising. Several of the German foundries arranged agencies in the United States and Britain, and exported a wide collection of types to them, cast on the American point system and trimmed at the foot to the Anglo-American height-to-paper – the trade being amply supported by persuasive specimen literature (from which the samples shown here are drawn). If the people in charge of the foundries had been no more than tradesmen, hoping to survive on their stocks of the mediocre display faces of earlier years, they would have failed to recognise the rapidly growing interest in typographic letter forms and the discriminating use of them. But as it happened, the principal foundries were conducted by people of taste as well as enterprise; they observed the buoyant mood of the time and responded by attracting the services of artists and designers who took to the task of designing type faces with enthusiasm and produced some remarkable results.

The display faces of the twenties and thirties can be considered as falling into groups, which can best be dealt with in ascending order of significance, beginning with two unusual faces created in France, of little importance to the printer but of some interest to the connoisseur. Bifur is, no doubt, one of the most impracticable types ever produced; but it is particular evidence of a

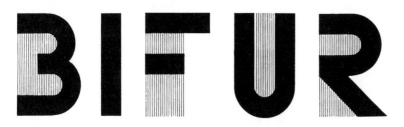

Bifur, by A. M. Cassandre;
Deberny et Peignot, 1929
The number of fine lines varied
according to type size

cultivated type founder, Charles Peignot, ignoring what are nowadays called market forces for the pleasure of allowing an artist to disregard the conventions of letter forms and to create an alphabet which obliges the reader to 'tune in' in order to get the message. (The Stop type face, of recent creation, works to a similar principle.) From the same source came the Peignot design, in which a theory, the 'return to origins', was the *raison d'etre* of

Alphabets

Peignot, by Cassandre;
Deberny et Peignot, 1937

an unorthodox type face. French typographers like it, but everyone else seems to think it suspiciously foreign. Those deviations from the normal – however fascinating to the observer – were of no practical value to the typographer, unlike another group which may be called 'decorative': types whose strokes are engraved or patterned in some way. Phosphor and Prisma, basically sans-serif, and Narciss, an old style, were inlined; so was Adastra, an italic. Vesta was an alphabet of capitals with a pattern on the main strokes; and the engraved letters of Lilith, especially the capitals, make a particularly rich effect. All of them became popular in Britain. They certainly added a fillip to print, especially on packaging, and it is a pleasure to see them turning up now and again. Those faces were from German sources, as were two romans: the fairly conventional Weiss Roman, which made little effect in Britain against the large sizes of Bembo, Garamond and others which Monotype were making available for in-house casting and hand composition; and the much more unusual Corvinus, a remarkably original treatment of the Didot

PHOSPHOR

Phosphor, by Jakob Erbar: Ludwig and Mayer, c.1926

MILANO

Prisma; Klingspor Foundry, 1931

No era in history
ADVERTISING

Narciss, by Walter Tiemann; Klingspor, 1923

Exhibition

Adastra, by H. Thannhauser; Stempel, 1928

WEEK-END
BOOK

Vesta; Berthold, 1927

Baltimore

Lilith, by Lucian Bernhard; Bauer, 1930

mode which became immediately successful when it was introduced in 1934, and was rapidly imitated by American and British type founders. Some of the characters of the light version of Corvinus were not well proportioned and there were ineffective tricks of detail; but the bold face was excellent. Corvinus was one of the most innovative types of the period.

There were other faces of German origin, distinctly individual in character, which might be called 'display romans'. The elegance of Locarno (called Eve in America), the dark forcefulness of Neuland, the strong personalities of Metropolis, Arpke and particularly Fanfare, which could only have come from a person and place thoroughly familiar with the 'fraktur' letter form; all of them were much appreciated as attractive accessories in typographic publicity work. Motor and Koloss, faces without serifs but hardly to be called sans-serifs, may be included here, as well as the American face Broadway, which was more subtle in its modelling than its Cotton Club image suggests. And perhaps this is the place for that interesting innovation, the stencil face,

Interiors of the NATIONAL

Weiss Roman, by E. R. Weiss;
Bauer, 1926

Minnesota Institute

American Printing

Corvinus, by Imre Reiner;
Bauer, 1929

The annual picnic NANTASKET

Locarno (Eve), by Rudolf Koch;
Klingspor, 1922

WHITE STAR LINE

Neuland, by Rudolf Koch;
Klingspor, 1923

ABCDEFGHIJKLMNO
abcdefghijklmnopqrstu

Metropolis Bold,
by Willy Schwerdtner;
Stempel, 1928

Eine Reise

Arpke, by Otto Arpke;
Schriftguss, 1928

DIVERSION
Cricket Club

Fanfare, by Louis Oppenheimer;
Berthold, 1927

EXCELSIOR

Motor, by K. Sommer;
Ludwig and Mayer, 1930

FROM THE
publicity R R

Koloss, by J. Erbar;
Ludwig and Mayer, 1923

INTERESTING

Broadway, by M. F. Benton;
ATF, 1928

Bright Moment

Futura Black, by Paul Renner;
Bauer, 1929

ALBERTUS

Albertus, by Berthold Wolpe;
Monotype UK, 1935

best represented by Futura Black. (On a day in March 1986 when a newspaper picture showed that Futura Black was in use on political display material in the Phillipines, the face was also seen in a London supermarket on a wrapper for watercress.) Entirely different from any of those faces – indeed, one of the most original and distinguished display romans of this century – was the Albertus type issued by Monotype in England, first shown in 1935 and developed with a lower case and in extra weights during the next few years.

The script letter was another form much exploited in the period. A. F. Johnson defined a script type as one 'cut in imitation of current handwriting ... the ordinary script in everyday use.'[9] Ordinary hand-writing is cursive – the letters run from one to the next – so the definition implies that this too must be an essential characteristic of a script type. Johnson said nothing on that point, but Stanley Morison, writing of the need for new script types, had expressed his own view quite clearly. He said the letters need not be joined[10] – which makes Johnson's definition inadequate, if not actually illogical. In fact, it is enough if a script type *suggests* handwriting; it need not be an imitation of it. Its characters may be tied or unconnected. The lower case will usually show some informal elements, and the capitals will always be more elaborate than those in an italic face.

Script types, which have a long history, had been particularly popular in the nineteenth century. The designs then were closely based on copy-book handwriting and used for the printing of personal stationery and for direct-mail circular letters before the introduction of typewriter faces. The common feature of the scripts was their regularity in alignment and proportion, and this was true even of those like the one called 'Scribble' that purported to represent a casual hand. All those older scripts were

Half-yearly Meeting

Scribble;
Farmer, Little and Co., 1886

Interior Decoration

Trafton Script,
by Howard A. Trafton;
Bauer, 1933

actually formal in style. There were a few essays in this manner in the 1930s; one of them, Trafton Script, which had a considerable vogue in publicity printing in Britain, was typical of a number of faces equipped with smooth curves and graceful flourishes to produce a pretty effect. An unusual product of the period was the script in which the strokes of the letters were of uniform thickness: the Kaufmann script, for example, and Gillies Gothic (designed by an American for a German foundry); in the first the characters joined, in the latter they were unconnected. But the

Apprenticeship

Kaufmann, by M. R. Kaufmann;
ATF, 1936

Winter Journey

Gillies Gothic, by
William S. Gillies; Bauer, 1935

Touring Association

Rhein Mosel

Holla, by Rudolf Koch;
Klingspor, 1932

Hampton Court

Legend, by F. H. Schneidler;
Bauer, 1937

most notable innovation in this class of design was the *informal* script: a type intended to make a word or title look as though it had been rapidly written in a distinctly personal hand. One of the best known was Holla. Its letters were unconnected so the type was 'typographic' in its behaviour, and it consorted fairly well with ordinary text faces. The same should have been true of Legend, an unconnected script of calligraphic character, most elegantly designed but of such strong individuality, especially in its lowercase, as to make it difficult to harmonise with other faces. Brush and pen scripts of the informal kind seem to work successfully only when the script is large and the other wording is set small.

The most influential typographic event of the twenties and thirties was the re-animation of two type styles of the past: the slab-serif and, more important, the sans-serif. Memphis and Beton were the best known of the slab-serif types created by German founders in 1929 and 1931 and exported to Britain and the United States. Their names are informative. Memphis refers to 'Egyptian', the early term for this class of type face. Beton, which means 'concrete' in English, indicates the industrial world

Radio

Memphis, by Rudolf Wolf;
Stempel, 1929

Parliament

Suspension Bridge

Beton, by Heinrich Jost;
Bauer, 1931

Master of French

for which the style was thought to be appropriate. Those two faces, along with others of the kind – Cairo, Karnak, Stymie and Rockwell developed in America, and Scarab in Britain – provided a new texture in publicity printing which has come and gone in favour over the years.

ROCKWELL gained by ABCDEFG

Rockwell; Monotype, 1934

ADVERTISING **typefaces display**

Karnak, by R. H. Middleton; Ludlow, 1931

The new sans-serif types arrived in three places – Germany, America and Britain – pretty much at the same time but from quite different motives. The Erbar, Futura and Kabel faces were created by German foundries in response to aesthetic ideas propagated by the artists and designers active in the modern movement in architecture and product design, who regarded the sans-serif letter as the only appropriate form in which to express the spirit of the time, and the arc, circle and straight line as the essential elements of that form. In the United States the Tempo face issued by the Ludlow company followed the style of the new German types; but Mergenthaler Linotype's Metro face (1929) was different and original. Its first version had something of the 'humanist' manner more clearly to be seen in the Gill Sans issued in Britain in various weights from 1928 onwards. (Linotype soon thought it necessary to produce alternative versions of some letters in the Metro face to 'modernise' it: that is, to Europeanise it.) The Gill sans-serif derived not from any theory about the purity and impersonal nature of geometric forms but from Gill's experience in the cutting of classical roman letters in stone, and from his observation of the sans-serif alphabets recently designed by his friend Edward Johnston for the London transport system.

All the new sans-serif types had several characteristics that pleased the typographers: capitals of natural width, an improvement on the dull 'square' capitals of earlier faces; and lower-case alphabets of evident quality – austerely elegant in the German faces, patrician in the Gill type. There was another useful attribute. Seriffed faces do not condense very well; even the condensed forms of Century Bold and Bodoni are unattractive. The

Central School

Erbar, by Jakob Erbar;
Ludwig and Mayer, 1926

Teknikko tai Konemestari
LOISTOHUONEISTON
Exposition de musique
CARNETS A SOUCHES

Futura, by Paul Renner;
Bauer, 1926

From the loving example
OF ONE FAMILY

American HEAVEN

Kabel, by Rudolf Koch;
Klingspor, 1927

DEMAND   **BORDERS**
If the printer   **Compact**

Tempo, by R. H. Middleton;
Ludlow, 1930

ABCDEFGHIJKLMNO
abcdefghijklmn 12345
ABCDEFGHIJKLMNO
abcdefghijklmn 12345

Metro, by W. A. Dwiggins;
Linotype US, 1929

ABCDEFGHIJKLMNOPQRS
abcdefghijklmnopqrstuvwxy
ABCDEFGHIJKLMNOPQ
abcdefghijklmnopqrstuvw

Gill Sans, by Eric Gill;
Monotype UK, 1928

sans-serif letter form is more amenable; it can be varied as to weight and width to a considerable degree without much loss of the identifying features in the basic design – though curiously enough the bold condensed versions of modern sans-serif faces are often less attractive than the condensed faces created in the early years of this century: compare, for instance, the condensed versions of Univers, Gill Sans and Helvetica with Stephenson Blake's Grotesques Nos. 7 and 9.

SURPRENANTE Univers Bold Condensed
les efforts

Gill Bold Condensed Gill Bold Condensed

National Brief Grotesques Nos. 7 and 9, Stephenson Blake

ORPLID Orplid, by Hans Bohn; Klingspor, 1929

The high quality of the sans-serif designs created in the nineteen-thirties raised the form from its former utilitarian status to equality with the seriffed roman. No longer was the sans-serif confined to the railway time-table and the headlines in the popular press. It was now recognised as having aesthetic value in its own right, and in spite of what some disapproving critics said about the mechanical look of the modern sans-serifs and their lack of 'humanist' attributes, professional typographers readily saw them as having personalities of their own: Futura being distinguishable from Erbar, and Kabel quite obviously different from either. More to the point, they saw the sans-serif as an essential item in the type face repertoire; as stimulating as, and sometimes more useful than, the seriffed faces. The regeneration of the sans-serif was certainly the most significant typographic event in that prolific period.

It was indeed a remarkable time. There was the increasing presence of the typographer in the advertising agency and in those publishing and printing houses that were conducted as much for quality as for profit; there was the rise of the trade typesetter able to supply settings in the new faces as soon as they came to hand; and there were the thought-provoking discussions of design in the typographical journals of the time. More than one writer on printing, referring to the revival of interest and practice in the 'laws of proportion, taste and workmanship' (to repeat Henry Stevens' words) has called the 1920s and 30s the 'typographical renaissance'. And as to type designs: it is not just nostalgia to regard the period, with its bounty of fine text faces from the composing machine makers and original display types from the founders, particularly the German, as the golden years of this century. That is a personal view. It was not Updike's. 'German typographic material, because it is so assertively German, is not in harmony with printing in the Anglo-Saxon tradition.'[11] His unwillingness to allow that the new types from abroad might supply a welcome garnish to the traditional typographic fare was not shared by Oliver Simon at the Curwen Press in London, who had a strong sense of that tradition and yet made good use of some of the new German faces. So did Francis Meynell, who could take tradition or leave it.

The five war years that began in September 1939 were not the time to issue new type faces; but some development work did continue, and quite soon after the war ended a new period of creativity began. Some very fine designs were issued in the 1950s and 60s. Linotype in New York issued several book faces that had been in process during the war years: Monticello, a revival of an admirable early American transitional face that since 1922, in its foundry form, had been familiar as the text face of Updike's *Printing Types*; Eldorado, a new type face inspired by an eighteenth-century roman; a stronger version of Fairfield, called Medium; and Primer, which was intended for educational book

A third type (which originated with Binny & Ronaldson of Philadelphia over a hundred years ago) is in design transitional between old style and modern face. For books where the old-fashioned air of Caslon would be too obtrusive, and yet which

Monticello, adapted from a Binny and Ronaldson face of 1812; Linotype US, 1946

Having established the general tone of your book in this form of two simple pages facing each other, you are free to go ahead and *embellish* the scheme to your heart's content.

Eldorado, by W. A. Dwiggins; Linotype, US 1953

Adverb Berry Craft Dumba
John Knack Lime Manner
Station Turner Uniform

Adverb Berry Craft Dumba
John Knack Lime Manner
Station Turner Uniform

Primer, by Rudolph Ruzicka; Linotype US, 1951

work. Linotype in Britain, pursuing its independent course, produced two good book types: Pilgrim, which had been designed by Eric Gill for a volume published by the Limited Editions Club in 1936; and Juliana, an original old style that came to be much favoured in Penguin paperbacks. Monotype in England introduced Spectrum and Dante, which were created in Holland and Italy respectively but were classic, not national, in character. And there was Eric Gill's Joanna, which he had designed in 1930 for use in the printing business he had formed with his son-in-law. While Mergenthaler Linotype's Corona news face was gaining great success in American newspapers, the English Linotype company created for the British newspaper field a number of news text and classified advertisement types which usefully enlarged the range of choice. It may be noted that all those post-war faces were made for mechanical composition ('hot metal') even

Since ev'ry man who lives is born to die,
And none can boast sincere felicity,
With equal mind, what happens, let us bear,
Nor joy nor grieve too much for things beyond our care.
Like pilgrims to th' appointed place we tend;
The world's an inn, and death the journey's end.

JOHN DRYDEN: *PALAMON AND ARCITE*

Pilgrim (originally Bunyan), by Eric Gill, 1934; Linotype UK, 1953

work of Hercules. Betwixt them long there was much contention. The Londoners indeed went bravely forward; but in three or four years I and my friends consumed many hundred pounds amongst the Plimothians, *who only fed me with delays, promises and excuses, but no performance of anything* [From THE TRAVELS OF CAPTAIN JOHN SMITH: 1593 to 1629].

Juliana, by S. L. Hartz; Linotype UK, 1958

THE TYPE known as Dante was first seen in an edition of Boccaccio's *Trattatallo in Laude di Dante* printed at Verona in 1954 by the Officina Bodoni. The design was made by the director of that world-famous printing office, Dr. Giovanni Mardersteig

Dante, by Giovanni Marderst Monotype UK, 1957

Printer's Specimen

Spectrum, by J. van Krimpen Enschedé and Monotype UK 1952–55

¶ Letters are signs for sounds. Signs for numbers and other things (like the sign for a dollar) may in practice be included, though they are not strictly letters (except as in Roman or Greek numerals & the letter signs used in Algebra). ¶ Letters are not pictures or representations. Picture writing and

Joanna, by Eric Gill, 1930; Monotype UK, 1958

though the manufacturers were actively engaged in developing photo-composition systems which would, some people thought, rapidly render metal typesetting obsolete.

The type founders were busy, too. Those who had an association with a composing machine company willingly produced text faces; hence the excellent Palatino book type and Melior, intended for newspaper work, both of which became available to Linotype users. And there were Meridien, an original design in the old style mode, and Sabon, an admirable essay in the style of Garamond, the result of an unusual joint undertaking by the Monotype, Linotype and Stempel companies in Germany. It was issued for machine setting in 1967.

Advertising
Hunting
Pyramids

Palatino, by Hermann Zapf; Stempel, 1950

Poetical works
Landscapes
Division

Melior, by Hermann Zapf; Stempel, 1952

STRATOSPHÈRE
Fantastique

Meridien, by Adrian Frutiger; Deberny et Peignot, 1957

On the Gold Coast of West Africa

Fundamentals of nuclear chemistry

Sabon, by Jan Tschichold; Stempel, Linotype and Monotype (Germany), 1967

A few decorative types appeared in the fifties. Three of them – Cristal, Flash and Calypso, from French type founders – may have been of very limited usefulness but they are interesting evidence not only of inventive design but of remarkable technical accomplishment in matrix making and metal type casting.

Script types had evidently lost none of their popularity in continental European printing. In a list of new designs by German foundries from 1945 to 1960[12] (and stated to be in-

SUPERBE

Cristal, by Remy Peignot;
Deberny et Peignot, 1955

FLORIDE

Flash, by E. Crous-Vidal;
Fond. Typ. Francaise, 1953

FORUM

Calypso, by Roger Excoffon;
Fond. Olive, 1958

complete) there were no less than thirty-two script faces, all of them original and attractive. Fifteen of them were available for export, cast on the American point system. Though script types were, and are, much less favoured in the United States and Britain than in Germany, France and Italy, it must be said that Mistral excited wide-spread enthusiasm when it was introduced from France in 1953. It is regarded as one of the most 'realistic' informal scripts ever created, though like other faces of distinctive personality, its popularity is intermittent rather than constant.

écriture manuscrite

Mistral, by Roger Excoffon;
Fond. Olive, 1955

Nameplate of a London restaurant in the Mistral type, which is normally a connected script

There were a few additions to the slab-serif class. Craw Clarendon, produced in America, the Consort face issued in Britain and the Clarendon made in Switzerland were all versions of nineteenth-century 'Egyptians'. Their revival was evidence of a turning away from the slab-serif designs created in the thirties, and it probably accounts for the fact that the Schadow face, designed in 1938 and extended in 1952, was not much noticed in Britain and America, though it was, and still is, one of the most original designs in the slab-serif mode.

A particularly interesting feature of typographic convention in the second half of this century was a new trend that occurred in the fifties in regard to the sans-serif. In the early years of the period Mergenthaler Linotype were developing the Futura face, under the name Spartan, into a considerable family of variations so that it became the most widely known sans-serif type series in the United States. At the same time the Gill Sans faces had a

Edgar Allan Poe

Craw Clarendon,
by Freeman Craw; ATF, 1955

BEAUTIFUL
Peak District

Consort (original c.1845),
revived by Stephenson Blake,
1956

Buildings

Industria

Haas Clarendon, adapted by
Hermann Eidenbenz: Haas, 1951

Rheinische

Schadow bold, by Georg Trump;
Weber, 1938

few years' popularity in Britain. In Switzerland, though, typographers had turned away from 'designed' sans-serifs and
formed a preference for 'grotesques' of the late 1890s, in the
belief that their impersonal character was appropriate for the
austere and mathematically regulated style of typographic design
they had developed. In response to this change of view the Swiss
foundry Haas revived and revised an earlier sans-serif and called
it Helvetica. The German foundry Bauer produced a very similar
type called Folio. And Monotype in England revived two faces of
the early years of this century, Series 215 and 216, which soon
overtook Gill Sans in the typographers' favour. This shift of
preference from the geometrically elegant Futura to the 'industrial' style of sans-serif, chiefly Helvetica, was a trend that

Une Course
Cathédrale

Helvetica, adapted by
Max Miedinger; Haas, 1957

CDEFGH **CDEFGH**
abcdefgh **abcdefgh**
ijklmnop **ijklmnop**

Folio, by K. F. Bauer
and Walter Baum; Bauer, 1957

Fashions change

Monotype Series 215

Fashions alter

Monotype Series 216

was observed in America, where several home-grown News and Trade Gothics returned to popularity. If this were a fully detailed history of typographic events in the twentieth century instead of a broad outline, it might seem reasonable to place this liking for such impassive type faces in a wider context, and see it as one more sign of the erratic aesthetic values of the era; the common-

Trade Gothic with **Bold**

Trade Gothic, Linotype US, 1948

BANQUEROUTE
une reproduction

Univers, by Adrian Frutiger; Deberny et Peignot, 1957

ABCDEFGHIJ
abcdefghijk

Antique Olive, by Roger Excoffon; Fond. Olive, 1962

Eurostile

Eurostile, by Aldo Novarese; Nebiolo, 1962

Watchmaker
Gabinete
Designs

Optima, by Hermann Zapf; Stempel, 1958

place being elevated to undeserved status and favour. However, there were some sans-serifs of real originality and merit: Univers, issued in France in 1957, a design of more subtlety and refinement than the industrial faces; the attractive Antique Olive, also French in origin, with its minimal ascenders and its curious curves; Eurostile from Italy, its curves disguised as rectangles; and Optima from Germany, universally admired as one of the most distinguished type designs of the century.

During the 1970s photo-composition systems developed rapidly, and the manufacturers of them had to face the task of providing the purchasers with the type faces they needed. As had happened when mechanical composing machines were introduced at the end of the nineteenth century, what the publishers and printers wanted was what they were familiar with, so the machine makers' first task was to reproduce on film font or disc the Baskerville, Bembo, Bodoni, Garamond, Times Roman and other well-known staples of the typographic diet. The long-established composing-machine makers understood very well how to produce type of the same high quality that they had achieved in metal type. The new manufacturers had no such experience and some of them evidently had no perception; the miserable appearance of their versions of classic types, the letters badly proportioned and unevenly spaced, is still to be seen occasionally in low-grade printing. Then, quite soon, there began a notable change in the type face scene: not the introduction of a new class of design but a change in quantity, a rapid proliferation of type faces offered to the typesetter and printer. It seems unnecessary to particularise them here: the types, and their designers, have been extensively publicised in recent years, and typographers are much more aware of their provenance than they are of the types of earlier years. But it may be useful to relate the *reason* for the change, and its consequences.

In the days of metal type and mechanical typesetting the development of a new type face involved a number of precision engineering operations for each character in each size of the design: a slow process and a costly one for the manufacturer and, inevitably, for the printer. The nature of the design was an important factor in the decision as to whether or not it should be produced. A design of obviously limited utility, like Bifur or Calypso, could only be indulged in as an unusual 'passenger' in the list if there were a number of work-horse faces earning enough to support it. The aesthetic quality of the design was important, too; an inferior design might become an expensive mistake. In specimen books issued before about 1960 there were usually some faces of little interest but few that were actually unworthy. The same cannot quite be said of the present state of affairs.

The reproducing of a type face by electronically digitising the characters, for storage on some form of adjunct in a computerised output system, is a comparatively rapid method of production, and computer-aided design devices are much in use to facilitate the creation of several weights of a basic design. Taking advantage of these methods, and noting that trade typesetters like to impress typographers with the number of faces they can offer, some machine manufacturers have increased their list of available faces to a bewildering extent. They have acquired additional designs from individual designers in the traditional way, but also from two particular sources: the makers of dry-transfer ('rub-down') lettering, and the studios that have been set up in recent years to make a business of supplying new type designs to manufacturers under licence. In principle, that ought to be beneficial to everyone. Certainly, some of the new faces that have been issued in the past few years are attractive and work well, and a few of them are excellent by any standard. But in those sources of supply the commercial compulsion to issue numbers of new designs frequently has evidently been stronger than the taste of those responsible for them. More has meant worse. The number of mediocre designs issued is depressingly high. Some of the faces are re-workings of types which first appeared at the turn of the century, when *art nouveau*, inventive and stimulating as it was in the decorative arts, was almost totally dismal in its effect on type design. And there are newly-designed faces in which the designer has employed such crude devices as soft-edge treatment of serif form, graph-paper structure, enlarged x-height, and so on, as the means of producing something 'different' – as if novelty were ever sufficient justification. Rather more reprehensible is the process of taking a type face created by a distinguished designer of the 1930s, re-shaping some of its characters and expecting acclaim for doing so. To say that digitising a design for laser-made output in medium or low resolution requires discreet simplifying of details may be justified in some cases; but to make radical changes in the character shapes while retaining the name of the original design is disrespectful, to say the least.

Inferior type designs ought to be still-born; but they appear in print because new type faces are projected at typographers with considerable blandishment, which evidently succeeds in its effect on those who have not yet learnt to resist the publicity, and form their own detached and level judgement of new designs. Yet typographers are the only people who can influence the suppliers of type faces; not just by refusing to use inferior faces but by expressing their views in print. For that a forum is needed: a journal of typography, independent of commercial interest or influence, in which type designs, good, bad and middling, can be candidly evaluated and discussed. It is an ideal unlikely to be realised. Genuinely independent and altruistic journals existed in the past, and occasionally included a critical assessment of a new type. A fine example was *Signature* (which at first puzzled one reader short of Latin by calling itself a 'quadrimestrial'). Its issue of November 1936 contained Harry Carter's review of the Fontana type[13], a perfect piece of detached and expert appraisal. Two other journals, *Typography* and *Alphabet and Image*, included occasional showings and comments on new types, but like *Signature*, only such designs as the editor thought had a high degree of merit; a survey of *all* the types issued in the period was not to their purpose. Those journals had a comparatively short life. There were only eight numbers of *Typography* issued in 1936 to 1939, and the same number of *Alphabet and Image* in 1946 to 1948. *Signature* began in 1935 and ran to fifteen numbers; a new series of eighteen numbers appeared from 1946 to 1953. The three journals, published in London, were each created by a cultivated printer and his friends, devoted to good printing in all its forms; and the same is true of the admirable *Printing &*

Graphic Arts which began to be issued from Lunenberg, Vermont, in 1953 and published its thirty-eighth and final number in 1965. The gratitude of their readers for what was done is matched by regret that there was not more. Exhaustion of finance or editorial energy, or both, was the usual cause of termination; but if by happy chance an ardent typophile, suddenly rich, chooses to publish a regular review of current typography, with an independent and clinical view of the latest work of designers of type and print, he should know that the task will require much effort, will produce little or no financial gain, but might have a salutary effect on the typographic scene that will be its own reward.

Mentors

The typographic sphere has had its leaders of knowledge and opinion, and books on typography and the graphic arts now fill a considerable amount of shelf space. Of those written since 1950 many are useful, but they supplement rather than replace the comparatively few works that were a vital feature of the typographer's education in the twenties and thirties. The fact that facsimiles of some of those older works have been issued in recent years is only partly due to the collector's harmless pride in possession for its own sake. It is chiefly due (one hopes) to the realisation that, as in other fields of design, a sense of values needs a basis of knowledge, and for that it is necessary to have a close acquaintance with the work of writers of the first half of this century, and to accept that their occasional inadequacies and errors are interesting and even valuable – a discovered error being sometimes more thought-provoking than the mere truth of the matter.

T. L. De Vinne: D. B. Updike: Stanley Morison

To inform themselves of the craft of type composition aspiring typographers in Britain in the thirties were still finding value in such works as *Printing: a practical treatise*, written by Charles Jacobi, manager of the Chiswick Press, and *Practical Printing* by John Southward, an editor and technical journalist. Both were issued in several editions in the early years of this century; and though they were decidedly dull in their appearance they were thorough and reliable in their descriptions of the nature of type, the rules of composition and proof-reading, and so on. In the United States the four volumes of *The Practice of Typography* by Theodore Low De Vinne[1], the eminent printer, had rightly been admired for similar reasons. Southward and De Vinne were concerned with the practicalities of printing, the craft of typesetting and the technique of press work, not with design in the creative sense of the word. Southward lectured on 'Art in Book Printing'[2] but did not in fact go much further than criticism of the slip-shod quality of the work of the time. De Vinne's paper on 'Masculine Printing'[3] (not an anti-feminist tract!) was a plea for simple un-demonstrative printing in place of the over-decorated work – all fancy type faces and curly rules – which was in vogue at the beginning of this century. No doubt Carl Purington Rollins was right to note De Vinne's aesthetic limitations[4]; but De Vinne did have a particular interest – the history of type designs. His *Historic Printing Types*[5] was the outcome of a great deal of diligent study in public and private libraries, including his own. In

London, the type founder Talbot Baines Reed spoke with knowledge and feeling on the same subject a few years later.[6] But it was another printer, Daniel Berkeley Updike, whose work was to be most significant. His *Printing Types, their History, Form and Use*, published in 1922 as an expansion of the lectures he had given at Harvard, was immediately recognised as indispensible by the typographers of the twenties and thirties. Harry Carter, reviewing the second edition (1937)[7], remarked that 'Updike on Printing Types has been very influential; it would not be fantastic to call the last fifteen years of typography the Updike Period.' A reading of the history of a subject does not automatically guarantee an understanding of it, especially if the subject is largely aesthetic in its nature. But to his account of the origins of type designs Updike added his opinions of them, and it is his comments and judgements that stimulate the reader and provoke thought. Disapproval, too, at times. Harry Carter criticised Updike for being too subjective about national character expressed in print: for example, for commending the Anglo-Saxon tradition without recognising that some of the types he attributed to Caslon were actually Dutch; for over-praising Spanish printing; for approving sixteenth-century French types but failing to greet them in books printed by the Elzevirs of Amsterdam; and for being too dismissive of German work. Nevertheless, he recognised that *Printing Types* 'is delightfully readable from beginning to end'. It is an influence that every typographer should experience – with due attention being given to the notes at the end of the work and to the fact that the author had little to say about the type faces that had been issued since the first edition. It must be said that the two substantial volumes of *Printing Types* are a pretty long stretch. A. F. Johnson's *Type Designs*[8] is a useful short study, though with few of the comments and opinions that in Updike are as illuminating as his facts.

Updike's *Printing Types* is chiefly concerned with type faces of the past and the books composed in them. Those were two important interests of Stanley Morison, too. He had others – his writings and lectures embraced early calligraphy and the history of the English newspaper – but the history of letter forms, and the research and scholarship that attaches to it were his particular field of interest, at least until the mid-forties. He deployed his knowledge and judgements in addresses to many societies and articles in numerous journals. His prose style sometimes lacked the easy clarity of Updike and others (though his letters were lively and enjoyable), but the reader was never in doubt about Morison's authority. For the typographer, perhaps, his most influential printed works were the volumes of *The Fleuron* to which he contributed in the twenties (it is a good library that possesses them), and *A Tally of Types*[9], first issued privately in 1953 and then published for general sale in 1973, after his death.

The new edition had an unreliable enlargement of Morison's original introduction but the advantage of additional material by other authorities. Its account of the types introduced by Monotype in Britain in the inter-war years is essential reading for every serious typographer.

Morison's *First Principles*

Stanley Morison's eminence in typographic research and scholarship is unquestioned. His ability as a designer of impeccable if always austerely conventional title pages was impressive, and his occasional excursions into commercial designing, as in his formula for the Gollancz book jackets, were fascinating and inimitable. But when he attempted to act as a preceptor of the 'laws' of typography the outcome did not always equal his intention.

The seventh and last volume of *The Fleuron*, which was published in 1930, contained his 'First Principles of Typography'[10]. Nowadays it would seem futile to suppose that there are common design elements in print, because of the sheer variety of it: the only thing common to a dictionary, a bible, a novel and a gardening handbook being their physical form, not their appearance. And the same applies in other areas of print: for instance, to such disparate items as a fashion magazine and a political weekly, or a marriage licence and an income tax assessment form. But in 1930 Morison evidently chose to disregard the multifarious nature of print in his desire to evangelise on behalf of good typography, an intention which was warmly approved of by others of like mind. *First Principles* was reprinted in 1936 with minor changes in phrasing, and at several times in various places subsequently. It rapidly became a classic, venerated as if it were an authoritative gospel, an affirmation of the basic principles of good typography from which all typographers may obtain guidance. It is not quite that, because it deals only with book printing. This may have been due to a decision in 1924, when the second number of *The Fleuron* was published, that subsequent numbers should be restricted to book typography 'when we realised that the principles underlying book and publicity design had nothing in common'.[11] The fact that *First Principles* includes a statement that 'there is, of course, a very great deal common to both book and advertisement composition' appears to be a contradiction, until one notices that in the first quotation the subject is *design* and in the second it is *composition*. If Morison had confined the essay to a detailed disquisition of the principles of good type*setting* (as Jan Tschichold was to do for Penguin Books in 1947), instead of describing just some of them along with some of the anatomical features of a book (treating neither subject very thoroughly), the essay would have been what it was presumably meant to be – an effective influence for good on all typographers.

Morison habitually undertook more work than he could comfortably manage. At the time of preparing the essay (it was a re-writing of a contribution to the 1929 edition of the *Encyclopaedia Britannica*) he was not only editing *The Fleuron* and writing for it but was also engaged on a detailed study of the history of English newspapers for a series of lectures and, in addition, becoming involved in the consultative work for *The Times* that was shortly to lead to the creation of the Times Roman type faces. With more time to ponder the essay he might have recognised its inadequacies.

Its often-quoted maxim that 'typography is the efficient means to an essentially utilitarian and only accidentally aesthetic end' is a typical *ex cathedra* statement that, in its use of 'accidental' for the aesthetic aspect of a typographic work, must have puzzled many readers. (It may be no coincidence that Eric Gill, with whom Morison was well acquainted, also used the term, as *per accidens*, in a similar context in his *Essay on Typography*, which was being written at about the same time as *First Principles*.)[12] Even to assume that 'incidental' was intended does not clarify the point. The statement seems to ignore the presence of the typographer and the contribution he makes to the visual quality of the work as well as to its efficiency; it gives weight to the functional aspect but too little to the aesthetic. If Morison had asserted as a principle that the aesthetic aspect is *secondary* to the functional his definition would have been clear enough, though arguable as a generalisation.

Another misused word – in addition to Morison's persistent use of 'fount'* for 'type face' – is 'imposition', the printer's term for the placing of eight or sixteen pages in a particular relationship on a sheet so that when printed the folding will bring them into natural sequence. (Savage's *Dictionary of Printing* shows 153 different schemes of imposition.) In *First Principles* Morison, who had no practical experience of the work of a printing office, used both 'imposition' and *mise en page* to mean the positioning of the type on a page so as to achieve decent margins. The terms are not synonymous; only the second is correct. Imprecision in the use of words may not be important; but to go on to say, as he did, that 'good imposition may redeem bad composition' is surely dubious counsel.

Considering that one of the essay's firmest statements is that 'the typography of books . . . requires an obedience to convention that is almost absolute', the reader could justifiably expect that the conventions would be defined in reasonable detail. But the advice on margins, which says little more than that where possible they should be proportionate to the type area and allow

* Fount (font in the United States) was the type founder's term for the quantity and assortment of characters needed for a particular class of work.

room for the reader's thumb, is too vague to be useful. A basic working formula – for example, back margin 1, head 1½, fore-edge 2 and foot margin 3 – would have defined one of the conventions the author had in mind; and if he had acknowledged that such margins possess aesthetic value as well as efficiency then there, clearly set out, would have been one of the 'first principles' that 'non-printers may like to consider for themselves' – and modify as taste or circumstances require. The suggestion that when pages have to be set solid it may be an advantage to add space between the paragraphs, varying it if necessary, could only have been justified if a particular class of work had been named. Bruce Rogers had the right of it when he said, 'Uneven leading or extra leading between paragraphs may sometimes be necessary in a reference or other special kind of book, but for ordinary text it throws lines out of register, interrupts the continuity of the text, and offends the eye.'[13]

In a passage on the design of title pages, the description of lower case as a necessary evil – 'it should be avoided when it is at its least rational and least attractive, in large sizes' – is a prejudice more than a principle. About the preliminary pages in a book, it is said that they begin with 'Half-title or Dedication (I see no reason for including both)'. This can hardly mean that he thought them equally dispensable; but it is just as hard to believe that he thought the dedication may replace the half- (bastard) title and thus *precede* the title page. And there is the curious notion that in a novel the list of chapters, if there is one, can reasonably *face* the title page. (To place the list *on* the title page, below the title, as in Gill's *Essay on Typography*, would at least be logical.) Morison would have done well to consult William Dana Orcutt's recommendations,* which were published in New York seven years before *First Principles* appeared.

It is surprising that Morison made no attempt to revise or expand the text of *First Principles* for any of the reprints that were issued in his lifetime, so as to make it serve a wider audience. After all, in the year before it was written he had said, 'But there is another kind of printing . . . to which the familiar canons of fine book typography cannot possibly be applied.'[14] He was referring to sales promotion matter. And in 1936, when the first reprint was issued, he wrote, '. . . advertising has no analogy whatever with the printing of books'.[15] He must have been aware that comparatively few people were, or ever would be, engaged in the designing of books, and that a large majority of pro-

---

* 'Anatomy of the Book', in *The Manual of Linotype Typography* (New York, 1923). It was the subject of a symposium in *Books and Printing*, edited by Paul A. Bennett (New York, 1951), pp.160–8.
See also Oliver Simon, *Introduction to Typography* (London, 1945), chap. 5; Hugh Williamson, *Methods of Book Design*, second edition (London, 1966), chap. 12; P. G. Burbridge, *Prelims and End-Pages* (London, 1967).

fessional typographers would be occupied with forms of printed matter quite different in purpose and physical character from that of the book. If he had identified some precepts applicable to typography in general – for example, the functional and aesthetic significance of space in all its aspects – and added them to an edited version of the original essay, it would have gained in practical value. In an introductory note to the 1951 reprint he said no more than that 'the sections dealing with composition may be adapted to the design of newspapers and publicity'. In fact, a journalist-designer could hardly adapt to his columns such principles as that a line should contain an average of ten to twelve words, or that small type needs space between the lines; and a publicity typographer would find the recommendations far too limiting for the great variety of work he or she has to tackle. In the reprint, the advertisement typographer was directed to Morison's article 'On Advertisement Settings', written in 1936, in which he had argued that advertisement 'copy' would be read more attentively if instead of being set in ordinary text fashion the space between sentences was increased and the roman lowercase was interspersed with words or lines set in capitals, small capitals, italic, bold face, and even different sizes. He evidently thought that such variegated texture would captivate the reader. But those are the recognised means of expressing *emphasis* in print; and since print is the representation of speech, a reader encountering advertisements set in that way might think that he was being addressed in a distinctly peculiar fashion. Alienation, rather than interest, would have been the likely result if anyone had taken the idea seriously.

In 1962 Morison wrote a lengthy postscript for a German edition of *First Principles*. An English version of it was added to a reprint of the essay in 1967 (he died in October of that year). The postscript added nothing to the substance of the original essay, 'because the author's position has not changed and his reasoning still appears to him logical . . .'. It was simply a reiteration of his belief in traditional style and conventions in book design and his mistrust of alternative methods of presentation.

Everything that Morison wrote has some interest for the student, and *First Principles* is no exception. It should certainly be read, if only for its intention. It seems likely, though, that for the past half-century students of typography have regarded it respectfully as a kind of sacred tablet but have actually looked elsewhere, to less exalted but more realistic sources, for practical guidance in the fundamentals of good typography.

Gill's *Essay on Typography*

The first edition of Eric Gill's *Essay on Typography* was expensive and limited to five hundred copies. In 1936 a larger and cheaper edition appeared, and *The Times Literary Supplement*[16] thought it useful to have the work reviewed along with *First Principles*, which had recently been reprinted. The review's fatuous title 'Mr Morison and Mr Gill: Typographers at War' was probably not provided by the reviewer, who actually noted that the two essays had a similar drift. He observed that the eminence of the two men was undoubted, but their attitudes were different: 'Mr Morison is a conventionalist; Mr Gill an eccentric.' Gill was hardly that. Holbrook Jackson put it better when he referred to Gill as 'in the world but not of it'.[17] However, the reviewer (anonymous, as was the paper's custom then) was justified in saying that Gill was 'a provocative and irritating but, for that very reason, stimulating companion'. There was a lengthy note on the merits, if any, of unjustified type setting and some questioning of Morison's ideas about the preliminary pages of a book and of Gill's use of the ampersand and his unusual word breaks. It was all fairly mild, unlike Francis Meynell's review of Gill's *Essay*: 'It isn't an essay at all. It is a collection of nine scarcely related essays of which the third is called "Typography". A fair part of this essay is actually about typography ... but an unfair part is about industrial ethics, which obtrudes also into all the other essays.'[18]

Meynell went on to point out the contradictions in Gill's arguments on the moral aspects of art, industry, the hand and the machine, and he concluded that whatever Gill thought he was doing he was actually writing about the printer, not printing. As a young compositor at the time and eager for guidance, I cannot have been alone in finding Gill's *Essay* not up to expectation – its didactic style oppressive, its insistence on the banishing of ornament understandable as to book design but unrealistic elsewhere, and its final proposal, that letters should be abolished and replaced by shorthand symbols, merely silly. The fact that the *Essay* told the student more about Gill than about typography was tiresome rather than interesting. Did the *Essay*, then, even with Gill's respected name attached to it, have any influence at all? In fact there was one feature that did have some effect: its unjustified 'ragged right' line endings. To be sure, that method of setting received little attention in Britain at the time; it was dismissed by many as yet another of Gill's eccentricities, though he himself had been familiar with the method since 1925 when Robert Gibbings had used it for the text of *Samson and Delilah* at the Golden Cockerel Press, for which Gill was a collaborator. (Incidentally, both Gibbings and Gill understood, as some later designers have not, that the 'raggedness' of line endings must be

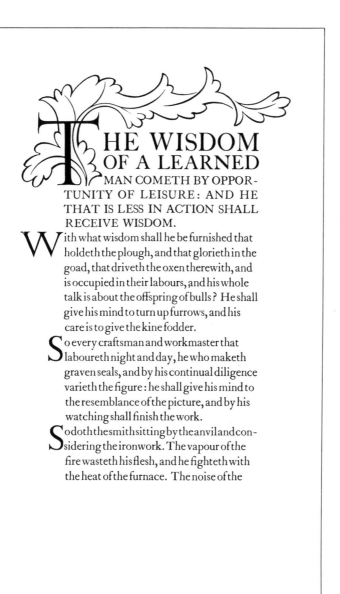

THE WISDOM
OF A LEARNED
MAN COMETH BY OPPOR-
TUNITY OF LEISURE: AND HE
THAT IS LESS IN ACTION SHALL
RECEIVE WISDOM.

With what wisdom shall he be furnished that holdeth the plough, and that glorieth in the goad, that driveth the oxen therewith, and is occupied in their labours, and his whole talk is about the offspring of bulls? He shall give his mind to turn up furrows, and his care is to give the kine fodder.

So every craftsman and workmaster that laboureth night and day, he who maketh graven seals, and by his continual diligence varieth the figure: he shall give his mind to the resemblance of the picture, and by his watching shall finish the work.

So doth the smith sitting by the anvil and considering the ironwork. The vapour of the fire wasteth his flesh, and he fighteth with the heat of the furnace. The noise of the

strictly controlled, with the aid of hyphenation whenever necessary, if readability and visual quality are to be maintained.) In the late 1940s, when asymmetric design was being explored and unjustified text setting was thought to be a concomitant of it, the pros and cons were quite seriously debated, and Gill's *Essay* was frequently used in evidence. That may seem odd and even naïve nowadays, when the method is familiar and unquestioned. But it was a debate about a design principle; and not only do principles have to be argued about before they can be understood and accepted, they have to be constantly in the designer's mind if his work is to survive his own appraisal of it.

Unjustified setting in a Golden Cockerel Press book, 1926

Beatrice Warde

Beatrice Warde (1900–69), an admirer of Gill and Morison's close colleague for many years, was a potent influence on students of typography during her long career. Her knowledge of letter forms was developed in the three years she spent as assistant to Henry L. Bullen at the ATF library in Jersey City. In 1925 she moved to London and wrote, anonymously, a fine article on the type-founding work of Pierre Simon Fournier,[19] to promote Monotype's revival of one of his text types. Under the name 'Paul Beaujon', the romantic nom-de-plume she invented for herself, she wrote for *The Fleuron* v her famous article on the origin of the various recent revivals of the so-called Garamond type.[20] The article was rightly applauded by those of academic mind and, of course, it interested those working typographers who read it, without disturbing their belief that the faces in question, although wrongly named, were perfectly useful and attractive type faces. Those articles became permanent contributions to the history of type designs, and they made her reputation. In 1927, at Morison's instigation, Monotype invited her to join the staff as editor of *The Monotype Recorder*, which she rapidly made into an important source of typographic information. The issues in which she and others described the type designs of Fournier, Cochin, Baskerville and Walbaum are highly valued in the literature of typography.

As an employee of a supplier to the printing trade she had to be circumspect in her opinions. This sometimes led to ambivalence. In an article on 'typographic transformations', a display of before-and-after treatments, she named the typographers and praised their re-stylings but went on to describe a 'problem of etiquette' in the relation between the designer and the printer. '... whereas it is always proper and helpful to show a craftsman *what effect* one wants, it is improper and thoroughly bad manners to offer to show him *how to obtain* that effect ...'[21] She thought the working layout that specifies all the details of line spacing, letter spacing and type sizes assumes that 'the compositor has not yet learnt the rudiments of good composing style' – a show of consideration for the printing office that contradicted the fact that the 'befores' illustrated in the article were the work of printers, acting as they thought fit, but clearly to unsatisfactory effect. When she wrote on a particular subject her writing was usually clear and graceful, though that was not the case with an address she gave to the Bibliographical Society in 1935 on the classification of book types[22]; its printed version was so laden with detail that Carl Purington Rollins said he could not understand two consecutive sentences in the whole article.[23] When her theme was a generalisation, such as the essay entitled 'Printing should be invisible', she cultivated a vivid prose style and indulged a fondness for metaphor ('the crystal goblet' as an image for typography) and rhetoric ('Friend, you stand on sacred ground' for a printing office), which was ingenuous but not to everyone's taste, though it charmed many. In the thirties she developed a facility for public speaking; and in a reminiscent interview many years later she said that what she had been really good at was 'standing up in front of an audience with no preparation at all and then for fifty minutes refusing to let them even wriggle an ankle.'[24] She gained that sort of rapt attention by a persuasive and fluent delivery, often with a ringing coda and dramatic gesture. She was indefatigable in her visits to schools of printing throughout Britain, where her influence on students was irresistible and wholly beneficial; she left them feeling grateful and privileged to be entering the typographic scene.

Paul A. Bennett

While Beatrice Warde pursued her notable career as a publicist in Britain, Paul A. Bennett performed a similar role in America, as the staff member of the Mergenthaler Linotype company responsible for the publicising of type faces. For many years he was a popular presence at most of the typographic gatherings in the New York area, and his genial voice was known to many throughout the United States. He wrote a certain amount, but was not a scholar or innovator and would not have claimed to be one. He was, however, a good editor; his *Books and Printing* is a useful collection of pieces by eminent people in the typographic world (the book has the unusual attribute of being composed in twenty-one different type faces). Bennett's talent lay in persuading others to commit themselves to print, through the medium of the Typophiles: 'a unique organisation which was never organised, but which has published a long list of excellent small books about books. It has no office, no staff, no sales force, no money. But it does have Paul A. Bennett.'

For many years Bennett gave much of his own time (and some of Mergenthaler's) to the service of the Typophiles. 'With only a glancing nod from Paul, writers write, artists draw, paper manufacturers give paper, printers print, and binders bind – all with eagerness and usually without a dollar of American currency in exchange.'[25] Thus wrote Joseph Blumenthal, the distinguished printer who produced a number of the Typophile Chap-Books, as they are called. Some of them are original works: for example, Rudolph Ruzicka's monograph on Bewick's engravings, and the accounts of their own type designs by Jan van Krimpen and Frederic Goudy. Others are compilations of essays on typographic matters by various hands. All of them are modest in physical scale but fine examples of (metal) typesetting, presswork and binding; and fortunately they continued to be issued after Bennett's death in 1966, under the care of the late Robert Leslie and latterly Abe Lerner.

Although Bennett was only one of the people involved in the conception of each work, he was its patient guardian; he devoted himself to following it through, often over a long period, up to the point when he could write the note that explained how the book came into being and described the voluntary efforts of the contributors to the project – author, designer, printer, paper maker and binder. Paul Bennett's value to American typography did not consist of research into the past, critical appraisal of the present or theories about the future of printing, but in the use of his warm personality and his power of persuasion to bring to fruition the work of others.

Jan Tschichold

In a letter to Updike in 1937 Stanley Morison remarked, 'One or two fluent Teutons are setting about to blow up the whole of English typographic tradition.'[26] He was evidently voicing his deep suspicion of artistic theories, especially those from abroad. In that letter he did not name the figures of dread he had in mind; but it is easy enough to guess. One of them must surely have been Jan Tschichold. Since the late twenties Tschichold's writings on modernist typography had had a great effect on designers in Europe, and in London an exhibition of his work had recently aroused the interest of many advertisement typographers and even some printers.

Jan Tschichold (1902–74) was born in Leipzig. He studied calligraphy and then turned to book designing. He became keenly interested in the graphic aspects of the artistic movements of the time: the anti-art Dada movement that had begun in Zurich during the First World War; the constructivists' theories about the significance of movement in space; the rigorous form of abstraction practised by the painter Piet Mondrian and expounded in the pages of De Stijl; the exploitation of photography, especially the photogram, by such vigorous personalities as Lissitzky and Moholy-Nagy – and no doubt he knew the latter's essay 'Die neue Typographie' in the catalogue of the Bauhaus exhibition of 1923.[27] (The essay was not really about typography but the value of the photograph as a concomitant of the printed word. More than that: 'It is safe to predict that this increasing documentation through photography will lead in the near future to a replacement of literature by film'.) Tschichold visited the Bauhaus exhibition in Weimar and was greatly stimulated by it, especially by the posters and other work produced in its printing workshop. At that time some constructivist artists were finding that their abstract compositions gained a special charge of energy if letters, the visual symbols of speech, were included along with the lines and geometric forms in the work. Such compositions were not typographic in the common sense of the word; they were works of art. But some of the artists did undertake commercial commissions: Piet Zwart for a Dutch manufacturer of cables; Paul Schuitema for a firm making weighing machines; El Lissitzky for a maker of inks, carbons and typewriter ribbons – his photogrammic designs hampered by the company's ugly nameplate.[28] That evidence of creative design, inspired by abstract art, was in sharp contrast to the dismal condition of most commercial printing, and Tschichold saw that the one could be employed to renovate the other.

In an article he contributed to the Leipzig journal *Typographische Mitteilungen* for October 1925 he included examples of typographic work by Lissitzky, Moholy and himself, and set down a series of guide lines as the basis of the new typography – one of them being a decided preference for the sans-serif letter form. He became a teacher of typography in Munich in 1926, and propagated the new doctrine in two important books: *Die neue Typographie*, a small volume published in 1928 and, in larger format, *Eine Stunde Druckgestaltung* ('a lesson in print design'), which came out in 1930. Its introductory text explaining the case for the new typography was followed by seventy pages of examples of a variety of printed matter – catalogues, stationery, advertisements, and newspapers – some of them in 'before-and-after' comparison. An English translation of its explanatory text appeared as an article entitled 'New Life in Print' in the July 1930 number of the London journal *Commercial Art*. The article began by saying that the new typography embraced the activities of some of the younger typographers working in Germany, Russia, Holland, Czechoslovakia and in Switzerland and Hungary. It pointed out that typographic design differs from architecture in that the form of a building may be determined by its function alone, whereas in typography there is an aesthetic aspect which must be clearly evident. And since typographic work is two-dimensional it was the new 'abstract' painters rather than architects who were the initiators of the new typography. The article went on to remark that pre-1914 traditional typography had only one style, the symmetrical, the most obvious example being the title page of a book. All printing, it said, had followed this axial style: newspapers, advertising, stationery and so on. Not until the post-war period (that is, after 1918) was it realised that these different areas posed quite different tasks to be dealt with separately and creatively by the typographer. The new typography, in which it was permissible to use 'every manner of plane relationship and every direction of line', was the natural reaction to the inanition of traditional centred typographic design. 'The extraordinary adaptability of the new typography to every conceivable purpose renders it an important phenomenon in contemporary life ... it is destined to form the basis of all further typographical progress.' The article, which was illustrated with examples of typographic work by Kurt Schwitters, Piet Zwart and others, ended with a statement of the main characteristics of the new typography, as set out by Karel Teige, a Czech designer: freedom from academicism; an understanding of the spirit of type faces and the use of them in accord with the character of the text; and the harmonious disposition of text and area by the use of geometric principles.

Criticism of symmetry and approval of asymmetry were not new. In 1928, the year of *Die neue Typographie*, W. A. Dwiggins had dealt with the subject in an unassuming way in his *Layout in Advertising*:[29] 'Symmetry is static – that is to say, quiet; that is to say, inconspicuous. Furthermore, it does not give much chance for the development of irregular areas – and irregular areas are assets ... But even irregular patterns need some kind of balance within the field of the design. Otherwise they would not have any organic structure at all. There is a kind of unsymmetrical balance that can be used to ballast the design and still give a chance for all the irregularity that I may desire. This irregular kind of balance

An early example of asymme typography designed by Will Bradley for the ATF *American Chap-Book*, April

has been known for a long time as the "principle of the steel-yard" – where a heavy weight near the fulcrum balances a light weight out on the end of the beam.'

The tone of the article in *Commercial Art*, and its assertion that 'the new typography, because of its utter rejection of any formalist limitations, is less anti-traditional than non-traditional', strongly suggests the kind of attitude that produced the distinctive changes in the fine arts during the nineteenth century: from neo-classicism to romanticism, to naturalism, to impressionism, and so on. Stanley Morison evidently saw it that way. In the printed version of a lecture he gave in 1937[30] he named Tschichold's published works in reference to 'the post-war movement of "new typography" (i.e. the romantic discovery by intellectuals of its appeal as a mechanical art)'. His use of 'romantic' was possibly his way of saying that the movement was

not only counter-classical but that its adherents worked from an
inner concept rather than an established model. But 'romantic'
seems quite the wrong label for the austere precision of
Tschichold's work at that time (and wrong, too, as a term for the
Futura and Kabel sans-serif types, which Morison had called
'romantic' in a letter written some months before the lecture[31]).
'Radical' would have been a safer term for the new typography
and it would, incidentally, have clearly reflected Morison's conservative attitude to design. In fact, he did use the word nearly
thirty years later, when he spoke of 'the risks that are implicit in
some of the radical theories of continental designers whose work
makes a great impression on English provincial minds.'[32] (By
'provincial' he presumably meant 'of another culture' and not
'naïve' or 'narrow-minded'.) There had never been any risk, of
course. By 1937 the wind of change from continental Europe had
already had a bracing effect on typography in Britain; and in the
United States designers were shortly to experience the benefit of
the presence of Moholy-Nagy and Herbert Bayer, and the stimulating ideas they had developed at the Bauhaus.

Although it was clear from the article in *Commercial Art* that
the new typography, inspired by modern abstract art, was a
consciously aesthetic movement, there was a cautionary note.
The article insisted that in any task there must be a clear realisation of purpose. Purpose must not be sacrificed to form. Form
must be the result of the work done, and not the realisation of an
external conception, a fixed idea – a fact that had not been
grasped by a 'whole troupe of pseudo-moderns'.

In the harsh political climate of 1933 Tschichold was deprived
of his post as lecturer in Munich and he left Germany to live in
Switzerland. His third major work, *Typographische Gestaltung*,
was published in Basle in 1935. It showed that Tschichold maintained his criticism of symmetrical layout as being inflexible and
lacking individual character, preventing dynamic effects in typographic tasks. He allowed that symmetrical work sometimes
served well enough for lines of unequal length, but on the whole
the rules of traditional typography contradicted the requirements of fitness for purpose. Non-symmetrical arrangements
were flexible and more effective for the functional needs of modern printing. The book went on to discuss type faces, with the
familiar preference for sans-serif as the best all-purpose type,
though the book types of the past were not excluded; and there
were firm recommendations for the correct use of indentation,
white space, colour, and much else. The tone was still didactic
but rather more permissive than in the earlier works.

The book was coldly treated in *Signature*, the most distinguished journal in British printing at the time.[33] The anonymous
reviewer (it was not Morison) observed that Tschichold, who
had already proved himself an influential teacher, was now less

dogmatic, but inconsistent in claiming that the new typography was functional because the abstract art from which it was derived, being non-representational, was 'precisely opposed to the objects of printing for use' – a curiously muddled judgement. A reviewer in *Typography*[34] was more appreciative; he thought that 'Any typographer, whether he can read German or not, should certainly have a copy of the book so that occasionally he can turn through its cleansing, clinical pages.' (A following issue of that journal contained an instructive article by Tschichold on the mixing of contrasting type faces). Neither review made any mention of the exhibition of his work that had been held in London in December 1935, which had certainly made an impression on the minds, 'provincial' or not, of the typographers and printers who visited it.

Tschichold's books were particularly well known in Switzerland, along with the work of Bayer, Moholy-Nagy and other 'pioneers of modern typography', as they have been called, and it was there that the influence of the new typography was at its strongest and its adherents most numerous. However, Tschichold himself began to turn away from its discipline and dogma, detecting in its motivation a disturbing parallel to the political totalitarianism of the time. His emotional distress is understandable; but it is hardly logical to equate an aesthetic style with political tyranny (though tyranny may, of course, *create* a style or enforce an attitude). There may have been a simpler reason: that after ten years' experience of the new typography he was tired of it, and needed a change to a less austere mode. Be that as it may, Tschichold's reversion to 'old' typography offended those, particularly in Switzerland, who had regarded him as the apostle of a faith; and it puzzled those in Britain who, after the 1939–45 war, were learning the principles of asymmetry and the virtues of sans-serif types as demonstrated in Swiss typographic journals and in the work of the Hochschule für Gestaltung at Ulm in West Germany, an important centre of modernist typographic design. But it was unreasonable to criticise Tschichold as though the new typography had the status of religious doctrine and he had defected from it. He had turned away from the style, not against it.

Tschichold's reputation remained high. In 1946 he was engaged by Penguin to restore the typographic quality of its books and to lay down rules for maintaining it – an event which had a beneficial influence on other British publishers, except for the few who were unaware of typography at all. In 1954 he was honoured by the American Institute of Graphic Arts, and there were other awards. In 1945 Ruari McLean had translated *Typographische Gestaltung* into English, but more than twenty years were to pass before it found a publisher. It appeared at last in 1967 (when the new typography was no longer new) under the title *Asymmetric Typography*[35]. The part that contains the comments on centred design has a footnote, not to be ignored. 'The gentle reader is requested to bear in mind that these were the author's opinions in 1935. Today I do not entirely agree with the statements in this chapter, no matter how effective they have been as the basis for the creation of a new style. The harsh rejection of the previous style, however, is the condition for the creation of a different one. J. T. 1965.' That seems sufficient justification for the emphatic way in which Tschichold had expounded the new typography in the early thirties; and it provides a reason for respectfully disagreeing with the distinguished practitioner of the style who said about the early writings, 'Tschichold's attempt to codify modern typography in this way was neither necessary or relevant. It was an endeavour which contradicted the spirit of modern typography and one which, if it had succeeded, would have done much to vitiate it and diminish its essential vitality and flexibility.'[36]

It seems unlikely that the graphic art of the constructivists or even their occasional commercial designs would have had much influence on printers and the new race of professional typographers if Tschichold had not used his experience as a teacher to explain the fundamentals of modernist typography in terms that could be understood in the printing office and the publishing house. Tschichold's propaganda for modern typography was necessary and valuable, and his codifying the elements of it, so far from vitiating typography, actually had a tonic effect. He can hardly be blamed for the fact that the recommendations as to choice and use of type that he expounded and the attitude to design that he encouraged, though salutary at the beginning, came to be intellectualised by its adherents into a style too austere for those classes of print whose function is to attract and beguile the reader.

Since 1967 when *Asymmetric Typography* was published a generation of typographers has grown up which knows about the 'new typography' by report more than by example. To judge by much of the work done today, many typographers have great need of the book: not only for its chapter on the use of space, in which the essence of asymmetry is explained, or for its observations on the refinements of good typesetting, or even for the fact that the book itself is an agreeable example of Tschichold's own designing (though it does not say so), but especially because it so clearly explains his purpose: to guide designers into a new aesthetic experience. His success in that task makes him one of the most influential figures in twentieth-century typography.

The typographic task

The caption to Peter Arno's celebrated *New Yorker* drawing of
the aircraft designer turning away from the mishap and saying,
'Ah well, back to the old drawing board', has entered the language as the perfect response to an experiment that needs a little
more thought. Experimental work is the tentative expression of
an idea or theory that has yet to be proved: hence the need for the
wind tunnel, and the boat designer's wave simulator. In the work
of the designer of an aircraft, a car or a yacht there may be a large
element of the experimental before the design can be sent forward to production.

For the designer of a river bridge matters are different. Within
limits, the visual character of the bridge may take one of several
known forms, all satisfactory as to function and appearance. But
there is a problem. How to support the bridge? The nature of the
ground on each bank must be discovered by trial borings; and
only when that information is available can the designer proceed
to solve the problem of supporting the span he has in mind.

Those are simple examples of two kinds of design work: the
tentative that requires proof, and the problem that needs a solu-
tion. In typographic designing the motivation is quite otherwise.
It is not experimental. Trials are not needed to prove whether or
not the words and pictures are comprehensible. Nor is typography 'problem solving'. There are no unknown factors. The
typographer acts entirely of his own volition. Knowing the size
of the area available and having been supplied with the text and
illustrations, he arranges the elements in one of the numerous
workable ways that come to mind and chooses the type faces that
he admires and considers suitable. In short, typographic design is
like dress design, a matter of *choices*, not experiments or
problems.

It would not be necessary to make these obvious points if
everyone understood that when people talk of 'experimental'
typography they simply mean unconventional design, and that
'problem solving' is an inappropriate term in this context. But
typographers, even eminent ones not normally inept in the use of
words, do use the terms, and the habit creates the suspicion that
the underlying intention is to make the typographer's task sound
esoteric and important. And that tends to mislead those new-
comers to the profession who have not yet acquired enough
experience to define and evaluate things for themselves. Typography certainly requires knowledge, ability and judgement; but
there is nothing mysterious about it.

To say that typographic designing is the making of choices is a
fair definition, but it is a short one and needs explanation. Jan

Tschichold's dictum that 'All typography is an arrangement of elements in two dimensions'[1] defines what is usually the typographer's first·decision, the disposition of the parts in the given area, with alternative arrangements duly considered and discarded. Then comes the choice of typefaces. If the piece is part of a whole, such as the title page of a book, or if it must conform to a style, such as a feature article in a newspaper, the choice may be prescribed; but it will be unconstrained in most kinds of publicity matter. If the result demonstrates liveliness in arrangement, so far as the logical sequence of the material permits, discrimination in the selection of types, and careful judgement in the spacing of all the elements, then the typographer has done well. If, however, some of those aspects are less than adequate it may be due to incompetence or lack of taste but may equally be due to the designer's attitude – which in publicity work often appears to be an eagerness to follow a fashion however much it militates against the effectiveness of the piece.

A fashion that has done much harm to the quality of typographic work ever since typesetting became computer-aided is the practice of reducing the space between the characters in text setting. Interference with the natural spacing of letters probably began not with electronic typesetting but with the inadequacy of the spacing guide on dry-transfer ('rub-down') lettering sheets and the impatience of the people using them, who took the easy course of ignoring the guide and setting the letters with only the minimum space between them, in ignorance of, or perhaps contempt for, the subtle balance needed by letters in their function as the components of words. Before long the mode was accepted into the aesthetics of advertising typography. The fashion was recognised by the manufacturers of electronic typesetting systems as a means of gaining the favour of trade typesetters and their typographer customers, so they contrived keyboard-activated commands to produce an automatic reduction of character spacing, to the satisfaction of any typographers with insufficient understanding of the nature of type and the reading process. Even some quite distinguished people have thought it necessary to be 'liberal' about the practice. Thus: 'In my opinion, closely set filmsetting may do its job perfectly well, when it is consistent and in character with its type face.'[2] (Since the space between letters is related to the widths of the letters themselves, the only kind of type face with which narrow spacing is 'in character' is a narrow one, such as a condensed sans-serif.) And, 'Very close setting is not necessarily wrong, any more than letter spacing; it depends on the words and the situation' – which is too vague to have any meaning. It is depressing that those remarks were actually included in a tribute to Jan Tschichold, who had such acute sensitivity to the value of space. If those who admire the practice were asked if they would tolerate a book (or, for that matter, a motorway exit sign) composed in 'minus' character-spacing they would surely answer 'No' – a tacit admission that the practice is not 'user friendly'.

In contrast, a few publicity and magazine designers in Britain, more interested in unconventional effects than in clear communication, have recently gone the other way, and developed a liking for over-lavish spacing everywhere: broad tracks of white between the lines of text, excessive letter-spacing of capitals, and even the letter-spacing of lowercase.

By the time these words are in print the fashion of misusing space may have been recognised as a mere aberration of taste and rightly abandoned. But fashions, even bad ones, are sometimes revived unthinkingly; a cautionary word seems advisable. Spacing in all its forms – between characters, words and lines, and between type and picture – is integral to the visual character of any piece of typographic work, and to its effectiveness in the functional sense. If a type face is properly made in the beginning (and it usually is) its characters are allocated side-spacing which will produce an even texture when they are composed into words. If the inter-character spacing is reduced on the typographer's instruction the interior whites in such letters as c, n and o become prominent, while the combinations of i with l and ll become darker, so that the texture of the matter is uneven and therefore less comfortable to read. On the other hand, if space is added where it does not belong the structure of the words becomes unnatural. Since most typographic work is done in the hope that it will be read (though there is never any guarantee of that) it is not very sensible of the designer to adopt practices that may repel a potential reader.

The typographer stands between the instigator of the work – the publisher or advertiser, say – and the public, in the role of mediator, 'a friend of both parties' (as the legal people say). The competent typographer serves the one by securing the attention of the other. The really good typographer does something more: he invests his work with such visual quality as to persuade us that (whether or not it is true) the words he is presenting to us are going to be a pleasure to read.

Not everyone who puts words into print on paper is a professional typographer. There is a new class of people who do so. They are the 'desktop' publishers, producing and distributing the reports and manuals generated in commercial and industrial organisations, the study papers put out by research institutes and universities, students' magazines, and much else. The common factors are low cost, modest quantity, and (not to be condescending) untutored effort. It used to be difficult to produce such work because the limited number of copies required (dozens, not thousands) made production by commercial typesetting and printing methods uneconomic. Modern technology has changed all that. The in-house employment of a compact system of keyboard, display screen, computer and laser printer has made the production of short-run printed matter easy, rapid and cheap, and many people are taking advantage of it. The quality of the print itself, even at the fairly low resolution of three hundred dots per inch, is not to be despised; and more refined output is available. The typographic quality of the work is another matter.

Desktop publishers who take the task seriously find themselves facing the same considerations that are the regular concern of the professional typographer: what size of type, how much line spacing, how to deal with section headings and captions, how to avoid 'widows', and so on. Ignorance of such niceties of good typesetting and of the disciplines of page make-up may lead to a result that will alienate the reader and thus defeat the object of the effort. Fortunately, help is at hand. John Miles' *Design for Desktop Publishing*[3] is an excellent guide in the basics of typographic design for the user of a personal computer; and Ruari McLean's *Manual of Typography*[4] is essential to anyone who aspires to professional standards. They are amongst a number of commendable works by writers of experience that enable the novice publisher to achieve a state of typographic grace.

Design: conservative and radical

The package designer works in three dimensions; the designer of
television graphics has the advantage of the illusory third dimension of depth. But in printed work the typographer has to arrange
the words and pictures in a flat area: that is, in two dimensions.
The elements are either arranged in the area symmetrically,
centred on an imaginary vertical axis equidistant from the sides
of the area, or they are disposed asymmetrically, balanced with
each other in some adjustment of the 'steelyard', to use
Dwiggins's term. The two modes are the fundamentals of all
typographic design – though some publicity designers seem unaware of the fact – and (unlike the sweet and sour in a Chinese
meal) the presence of both modes in a design, as in some of
Bernard Shaw's title pages, is inevitably incongruous. The two
methods of arrangement can be studied at their simplest in the
design of books and newspapers, and in connection with them
the merits of each mode have been much discussed; not always
convincingly.

In the book

The symmetrical style, often labelled 'conventional' and 'traditional', has been taken for granted but seldom actually
explained.

The early printers, like other manual craftsmen, must have
begun by doing things the simplest way. When the printer had
some lines of unequal length to compose for a title page or above

Naturæ præpo-
fitionū ex Pri-
fciano.

PARISIIS.
Apud Franciſcum Stephanum.
M.D.XXXVIII.

Involuntary asymmetry in a ti
page by F. Estienne, 1538,
shown in Stanley Morison's
Four Centuries of Fine Printin
(1924). The title is in a type to
large for the words, perhaps
because the smaller types wer
locked up in other work. If th
second and third lines had bee
centred the end-of-line hyphe
would have made the setting
even more awkward than it is

a new chapter, the easy course, familiar to anyone who has set
type by hand, was to place some quads (broad spaces) in the
composing stick, set the words of the first line, place the same
number of quads after them, and then add or subtract spaces on
each side of the words until the line was sufficiently full to the
page width. When the other lines were similarly set and the page
was proofed, the type sizes and line spacing may have needed
improvement but the *idea* of centering the lines was accepted
without question, because the visual effect it produced had the
same agreeable attributes of symmetrical balance and stability
as, say, the facade of a church; and, for that matter, the erect
human figure. In short, it would have seemed 'natural' to set lines
in that fashion; and since the style was easy to produce and
decorous in appearance it became a convention as a matter of
course. That practice of arranging the elements of the page on a
central vertical axis remained a firm custom which continued
unchallenged for over four centuries; and it has obviously been
the only possible way to arrange the type on title pages designed
by people with a liking for ornamental borders set from printers'
'flowers', in imitation of sixteenth-century book work. In the
twentieth century that sort of thing is obviously anachronistic;
yet Bruce Rogers was admired for his use of arabesque fleurons –
the kind described by Stanley Morison and Francis Meynell in
the first volume of *The Fleuron* (1923). Rogers usually applied
that 'period' style to literature of the past, so it can be said that it
was appropriate – although it looks incongruous on his title page
for *The Rime of the Ancient Mariner*, considering the date of the
original (1798), and its melodramatic subject. Even more inept
was an English publisher's use, in 1926, of Fournier's ornaments
and his pretty decorative capitals for a series of H. G. Wells's
novels. In that eighteenth-century costume *The Island of Dr
Moreau* cannot be taken seriously.

In his *First Principles of Typography* Stanley Morison remarked that in a book 'the preliminary pages offer scope for the
utmost typographical ingenuity'; and in the postscript to it he
wrote, 'The right order for printing a given piece of writing may
sometimes benefit from intuition or imagination.' That show of
tolerance for the unconventional and inventive seemed to suggest
that he would willingly allow asymmetric design into the title
page and preliminaries in a book: in its sophisticated form, where
the elements are deftly placed and balanced across and down the
page, or in its simpler form, usually called 'flush left', where the
lines extend flag-like from a single invisible vertical. But
Morison's tolerance was not real. A little later in the postscript
he said about the typographer, 'For him as a designer of books, it
is above all things necessary to be orthodox ...' Although he did
not condemn asymmetry by name his use of 'orthodox' and such
terms as 'reason' and 'tradition' must mean that in his mind the

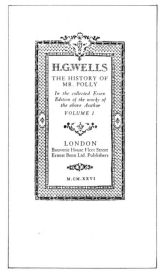

Wells farrago

symmetrical was the only acceptable sort of arrangement: any other was not only not to his taste but was somehow reprehensible.

Morison's views on book design were conservative and simplistic; but because of his eminence his opinions, expressed as dogma, have been influential. Fortunately, they have not prevented other views on the matter.

An alternative view of book typography was expounded in *Books for Our Time*, which was published in 1951 in connection with an exhibition held in New York. Its committee members were Marshall Lee, Merle Armitage, John Begg, S. A. Jacobs and Ernst Reichl who, along with Herbert Bayer and George Nelson, contributed essays to the book which had the effect of a manifesto dedicated to 'modern' book design. 'It seems incongruous that today ... we should yet strive to design books with conventions perfected centuries ago. Our aim should rather be to evolve a contemporary expression, related to our world as the traditional style was to its.'[1] (Jan Tschichold had once used similar terms about the 'new' typography of the 1930s: he wrote that it was needed to 'express the spirit, the life and the visual sensibility of its day'[2]). Like others of the kind, the essays in *Books for Our Time* were stronger on the polemical than on the judicious, perhaps because the authors felt an emotional need to confront adherents of the traditional way like T. M. Cleland, P. J. Conkwright and others. It was not sensible of Marshall Lee to assert that the exhibition marked the 'beginning of an era', when some of the selected books were over twenty years old. On the other hand, it was reasonable to say 'We see tradition as part of a designer's background rather than as a set of conventions to which he must conform'; and it was fair comment at that time to observe that 'The iron grip of tradition and its staunch defenders have effectively kept the creative designer away from British books.'

Books for our Time was by no means iconoclastic, but in presenting its theme – off with the old, on with the new – its authors made several errors of judgement. It was unwise to generalise about the design of books, as though their differences in subject and purpose have no significance. The statement that 'The book designer of today conceives of the book as an extra-dimensional form existing in time as well as in space' was so cryptic as to strain the reader's patience. To call it 'incongruous' to use 'conventions perfected centuries ago' was to historicise the subject: to imply that centred matter on title pages and margins organised in the traditional way represent past modes of thought and are therefore sterile archaisms. The fact that the style was developed long ago is of no consequence; it is its persistence that is relevant. The simple fact is that the conventional centred style is *comfortable*. It demands no effort from the reader; and from the typographer it requires a sufficiency of taste but nothing much in the way of invention. Indeed, taste – sensitivity as to choices – is the chief attribute of Bruce Rogers and his kind. Discrimination in the choice and disposition of typographic material is essential, of course, but something more is often desirable: not only elegance in the handling but a visual allusion to the subject of the work. And that is where the authors of *Books for our Time* had a point. They may not have chosen the best way to explain themselves, but what they were doing was making a claim for a greater expressiveness.

In that they were right. Books are not simply objects to be used, with function as the sole attribute to be considered. To quote Saul Bass: 'Often, designers tend to justify their designs by pointing to their "practicability" (the legibility of reading matter, the economy of structure, the efficiency of use, etc.). I am always chagrined that such emphasis is given to "functionalism" in this narrow sense. The battle for functionalism was won some time ago.'[3] Books are, or should be, things to admire and enjoy, for their appearance as well as their content. *Dignified* and *tasteful* need not be the only adjectives of approval. *Stimulating* should be just as legitimate a response to the designer's contribution to the book, when it reflects and enhances its subject and has not been imposed upon it according to a manifesto about design in general. Symmetry and asymmetry are of equal value to the designer. He may decide that a political biography, say, is best presented in plain centred style; but for many other subjects, not excluding the novel, 'typographical ingenuity' seriously applied in the title and preliminary pages may be a definite asset. It goes without saying, however, that any designer who regards an unconventional style as a licence to kill, and destroys the sense in favour of the pattern, is no friend to the reader and deserves to see the book remaindered.

In their claim for a contemporary approach to book design the proponents of *Books for our Time* did not go so far as to pass judgement on the type faces that could or should not be used by a modern designer. They did not repudiate Garamond, Janson and Baskerville, for instance, just because those types had been born in the distant past. No doubt they recognised that not only do few readers know anything of the provenance of a type face but that the typographer, who does know it, leaves that knowledge in the back of his mind and is concerned only with the character of the type and with its practical attributes of proportion, colour and so on. To have asserted that a book written and produced in the twentieth century must be composed in a type of its own time would have implied that Granjon or Janson, say, were not allowable for Philip Roth's new novel and, by the same argument, Aldus, Electra or Spectrum were out of order for a new edition of *Gulliver's Travels*.

Asymmetric
title pages:
by John Trevitt,
1962 (left), and George Mackie,
1970 (right)

STANLEY
SPENCER

a biography by
MAURICE COLLIS

London: HARVILL PRESS

Behind | Appearance

A study of the relations between
painting and the natural sciences
in this century

C.H.WADDINGTON FRS
Edinburgh, *at the University Press*

Two ways with *Ulysses*: by Ernst Reichl, 1934, New York,

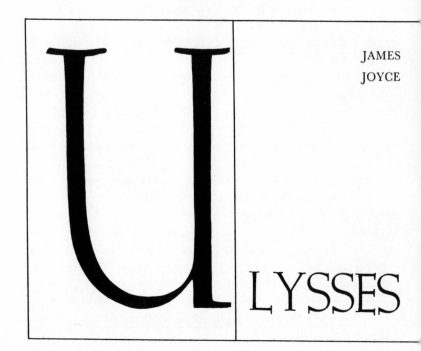

JAMES
JOYCE

ULYSSES

****EDITED AND
****DESIGNED BY
1938 **MERLE ARMITAGE**
WITH ARTICLES BY

GEORGE
GERSHWIN

PAUL WHITEMAN ★ OLIN DOWNES ★ WALTER DAMROSCH
GEORGE GERSHWIN ★ MERLE ARMITAGE ★ OTTO H. KAHN
ARNOLD SCHOENBERG ★ WILLIAM DALY ★ HAROLD ARLEN
OSCAR HAMMERSTEIN II ★ ISAMU NOGUCHI ★ DAVID EWEN
NANETTE KUTNER ★ LESTER DONAHUE ★ ISAAC GOLDBERG
ERMA TAYLOR ★ GILBERT SELDES ★ J. ROSAMOND JOHNSON
RUDY VALLEE ★ LEONARD LIEBLING ★ ALEXANDER STEINERT
ALBERT HEINK SENDREY ★ JEROME KERN ★ DuBOSE HEYWARD
HENRY A. BOTKIN ★ SAM H. HARRIS ★ ROUBEN MAMOULIAN
EVA GAUTHIER ★ FERDE GROFÉ ★ LOUIS DANZ ★ TODD DUNCAN
BEVERLEY NICHOLS ★ IRVING BERLIN ★ S. N. BEHRMAN
GEORGE ANTHEIL ★ IRA GERSHWIN ★ SERGE KOUSSEVITZKY

PAINTING BY SIQUEIROS

L O N G M A N S ,   G R E E N   &   C O · L O N D O N · N E W   Y O R K · T O R O N T O

by the Penguin design staff, London, 1968

JAMES JOYCE

ULYSSES

WITH

ULYSSES: A SHORT HISTORY
BY RICHARD ELLMANN

PENGUIN BOOKS
in association with The Bodley Head

FRANÇOIS RABELAIS

Five books of the Lives,

Heroic Deeds and Sayings

of GARGANTUA and

his son PANTAGRUEL

Translated into English by

Sir Thomas Urquhart of Cromarty

and Peter Antony Motteux

THE FRASER PRESS · LONDON · 1970

Above,
A title spread by
Merle Armitage,
New York, 1938

A flush-left
title page by
Peter Guy,
London, 1970

In regard to the disposition of type on the page the authors of *Books for our Time* were not advocating Tschichold's ideas. He was not mentioned at all in the text and only one example of his work was illustrated, the well-known title spread in his *Die neue Typographie* of 1928. (By contrast, there were twenty-three specimens of Merle Armitage's book designs.) Although asymmetric arrangement was the style common to almost all of the 152 books shown in *Books for our Time*, the influence in them so far as there was one, was not the austere discipline of Tschichold or the 'Swiss style' but the relaxed and varied typography of advertising. To look for discipline in design and the use of centred and asymmetrical style we may turn to another area of print: the newspaper press.

In the press

Throughout the nineteenth century the page structure in newspapers was strictly single-column vertical. Even the great fire of October 1871 did not inspire the *Chicago Tribune* to break the mould, though its single-column lead-in heading on its front page consisted of fifteen decks and occupied over three-quarters of the column. Double-column headings did not appear until the last years of the century, and then only for a remarkable event like the fall of a government or the result of a battle. As Allen Hutt pointed out, war news was a great stimulus to the editors of popular newspapers.[4] The sinking of the *USS Maine* in Havana harbour in 1898 caused the *San Francisco Chronicle* to head its front page with a full-width two-deck banner carrying a strong emotional charge: its second deck read 'A Terrific Explosion Rends the Magnificent Machine of War and Brings Death to Hundreds of the Brave Fellows Upon Her'. Many years later Orson Welles in his 'Citizen Kane' was able to make dramatic capital out of William Randolph Hearst's provocative treatment of the Spanish-American war news in the New York *Journal*. And it was the First World War of 1914–18 that forced British newspapers to record the daily news with typographic means adequate to express the grim drama of the times.

Not until well into the present century did newspapers begin to recognise the increasing sophistication of advertisement and magazine design and discern that their own product needed visual improvement. A curious feature of news story headings in American newspapers in the first thirty years or so was the formalising of them into rigidly maintained shapes. There were several of them. In the *stepped* deck the first line was flush to the left but with two units of space at the right; the second line had one unit at each end, and the third line began with two units of space and ended flush to the right. In the *inverted pyramid* the lines were long, shorter, short; carefully calculated to make a broad taper. In the *hanging indent* arrangement the first line was full out to the sides of the area, and the following lines indented at the left and flush to the right. And there was the *full out* style, in which all the lines had to fill the column width. The headline writer forced to search for words that would precisely fit such

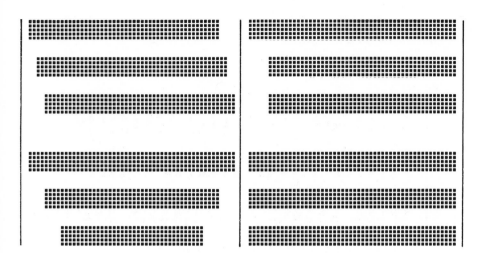

rigid requirements was not always successful; all too often the formula was only achieved with excessive space between words or space between letters.

With the exception of one or two popular papers that imitated American tabloids most British newspapers did not take to such formalised heading arrangements. They contented themselves with centred headings, derived from the 'title page' style of the early news-books. But the stepped and other formalised headings prevailed in the United States for many years. In 1917, when the *New York Tribune* engaged the typographer Ben Sherbow to re-dress the paper's headings, his innovations – the use of one type face only, Bodoni Bold, and the discarding of all-capital head-lines – were certainly original;[5] but he retained the formalised heading conventions, as if they had the status of an inviolable aesthetic principle. The *New York Times* still uses a selection of them on its news pages, which contrast sharply with its well-designed feature pages.

A new view of the subject began to be expressed in 1929, when John E. Allen, editor of *Linotype News*, Mergenthaler Lino-type's external house journal, used it as a medium to develop a series of innovative page treatments which in time had a good deal of influence in the American press world. He advocated three principles for news heading typography: the reduction of the number of decks in a heading to two, and finally to one only; the replacement of all-capital lines by lowercase (though he de-fended the American custom of giving all words except the minor prepositions an initial capital); and, most importantly, the sett-

Formalised heading structure: stepped, inverted pyramid, hanging indented, and full-out.
Some eminent American newspapers have evidently thought that such rigid shapes are essential for an authoritative appearance

ing of the headlines in the 'flush left' mode – i.e. the lines ranging vertically at the left but 'free' at the right. At about the same time, as it happened, Jan Tschichold in Germany was advocating 'asymmetric' typographic design, and he showed two specimen newspaper pages with flush-left headings in his *Eine Stunde Druckgestaltung* of 1930.[6] It is unlikely that the two men knew anything of each other's work. In fact, Allen had been influenced at first by an event much nearer home: the re-styling of the New York *Morning Telegraph* in 1928, in which some headings were

Flush-left headings look spontaneous but line lengths need careful control

This symmetrical style is less dynamic but line lengths are not so vital

set in the flush-left mode.[7] The term 'free style' has been much used to describe this form of heading treatment. It was certainly relaxed by comparison with the strict conventions of the formalised styles; but it was not as free, or as easy to write, as many people thought. An observer of the British scene wrote in 1953, 'What is it about flush-left headings that makes them so strongly advocated by knowledgeable critics but so seldom adopted by newspapers themselves? ... John Allen, Thomas Barnhart and other writers in America have pointed to the freedom the flush-left style allows in writing and setting, and to its vigorous impact on the reader. But the flush-left form of heading arrangement has its limitations – or rather, its special requirements. For one thing, it is easier to get a good effect in a two-line heading (one long line

Flush-left and centred. (These two specimens are composed in a headline face designed in 1987 by Shelley Winter and Walter Tracy at the request of *The Daily Telegraph*, which holds the copyright.)

and one a little shorter) that in a three-line deck; and a four-line flush-left setting is much more difficult to arrange successfully.'[8]

'Free style' is a mis-nomer. The flush-left heading may appear to be spontaneous − type-set just as it was written − but if the lines in the heading are to be properly proportioned with each other and to the column width the writer needs an alert visual sense and a mind well-stocked with synonyms for the rapid adjustment of line length. To avoid ungainly areas of white on the page the lines need to be about three-quarters of the column width; if they are less than that the white at the right will be unsightly. If there are several such, the page will look patchy and to the professional eye, uncontrolled. If one of the lines in an asymmetric heading is too short, the shape of the heading will be inelegant. In the centred mode the same line, with the white divided on each side of the words, might well be tolerable. The asymmetric heading style needs expertise that is not always available.

It is an interesting fact that from the design point of view news headlines are produced in quite the opposite way from the heading in a display advertisement. The advertisement typographer may do anything he likes with the headline wording the copywriter has given him, choosing type face, size and line length at will. In a newspaper (one run by professionals, that is, not the sort of 'free sheet' which in Britain is produced by people untouched by typographic knowledge) the paper's style manual specifies the form, type size and type face for the headings in every position in the paper, and the headline writer works to the rule. If he does not choose his words carefully the ill-fitting result may make the readers think the paper does not know how to dress itself.

Reading: research: reform

In a fit of depression a typographer might wonder if anyone will actually read the piece of work he has just completed, but he has no doubt that most of us *can* read it if we are willing to do so. Most of us; but not everyone. In 1970 there were thought to be more than three million illiterate adults in the United States,[1] and as recently as May 1987 a government department in Britain found that more than one in five of the long-term unemployed have difficulty in reading, writing, or simple arithmetic.[2] Those of us who read easily should count ourselves fortunate. In fact, we probably never give it a thought; or, if we do, we think of reading as we do of breathing – something that comes naturally. It does not. Reading is a skill: it has to be learnt, which means that it has to be taught. Teaching it is not a simple task. For many years educationists have been devising methods of teaching literacy, evaluating the methods and describing them in professional journals. And it is not only the teaching of infants that concerns them; older students are a problem too. 'Universities often complain that their undergraduates have been poorly prepared to undertake the reading involved in their courses.'[3]

Reading is what happens at the receiving end of the communication process. The transmission end was elegantly expressed by Edmund Fry in 1799. 'The desire of communicating ideas seems to be implanted in every human breast: the two most useful methods of gratifying this desire are, by sounds addressed to the ear, or by representations or marks exhibited to the eye; or, in other words, by *Speech* and *Writing*. The first method was rendered more complete by the invention of the second, because it opened a door to the communication of ideas, through the sense of *sight*, as well as that of *hearing*. Speech may be considered as the substance; and writing, as the shadow that follows it.'[4]

Educationists find it hard to agree on a definition of reading. One view is that writing is an encoding process, the action of representing language by symbols called letters; therefore reading is the process of *decoding* such symbols and converting them into language. A person performing that decoding process has learnt the alphabet and can recognise word formations. But is that reading? Is that person literate? Many psychologists think not, and insist that an adequate definition of reading and literacy must include *comprehension* of what has been read. They have made the reading process the subject of research, not only for the teaching of children but for the measurement of reading ability in adults, and they have devised testing procedures to measure comprehension and to examine the factors, including the typographic ones, that affect it. 'Legibility research' is a general term for these studies; 'legibility' being used in a broad sense because the studies include investigations into the *readability* of continuous text as well as the *legibility* of individual letters and numerals.

The amount of research has been remarkable. Surveys issued in 1969 and 1980 taken together include references to nearly 900 studies of one sort or another.[5,6] The layman looking into the subject finds it complicated by the variety of methods used by the researchers. One worker in the field had to say, 'For conventional prose there is still widespread disagreement about the proper means for assessing reading performance in a reliable and valid manner.'

The researchers' methods have certainly been varied, and some of them seem decidely remote from everyday life. The distance method, for instance, in which a printed test sheet is drawn away from the subject until he can no longer read it, is quite contrary to the natural habit of reading at a constant distance of about thirty-three centimetres. The measurement of eye movement or blink rate in relation to perception no doubt helps to explain the physical aspect of the reading process but seems unconnected with comprehension. And studies in the early years of this century which revealed that long words are more easily recognised than short ones, and that the first half of a word is more important for perception than the latter half, make one wonder what the response of journalists or copywriters would be to a request that they should write only in long words or words without a second half. As one researcher admitted, 'The scientific method, because it *selects* variables for manipulation and study, does not and cannot reproduce the complexity of reality.'[7]

It has been claimed that the purpose of research is to identify the limits beyond which the effectiveness of communication is reduced.[8] It is not a justification that will appeal to the professional typographer, who believes that effectiveness of communication is just what he has been trained to achieve. Nevertheless, he has been criticised for his lack of enthusiasm. 'Many designers and printers ... view the whole notion of legibility research with suspicion ...'[9] Before deciding on the fairness of the charge it will be worth taking time to consider the kind of thing in which designers and printers were thought to be failing in attention.

Researchers investigate; reformers seek to rectify. Some of them have asserted that the English-speaking world is disadvantaged because the language itself, especially its spelling, is illogical, which hampers learning; and uneconomical, because many words have more letters than are necessary to represent their sound in speech. Others have criticised the alphabet we use in writing and printing as being too limited, providing only an approximation to the language as it is spoken. The remedies proposed have been as various as they have been numerous.

The English language is a remarkable hybrid derived from many sources. It began as a vocabulary accumulated from the dialects of the invaders of Teutonic and Scandinavian origin who settled in England from about the middle of the fifth century A.D., after the Romans had departed. It is usually called Anglo-Saxon; we get our *th* sound from it, and the verb ending *ing*. In the course of time men of vision created a literature, and adopted letter forms in which to write it. After the Norman conquest in 1066 a large number of French words were added to the language (*jargon*, which meant the twittering of a bird, is one of them). The Norman scribes introduced J into the alphabet and eliminated the Anglo-Saxon letter which had stood for the *th* sound. At the same time there began a profound change in the pronunciation of vowels. The relationship between word-sound and its written version became capricious, and irregularities multiplied. Spelling was for a long time a pretty arbitrary business, as Chaucer's *Canterbury Tales* demonstrates. Frederick Bodmer thought the breach between spelling and speech was widened by classical scholars whose views on word origins were often mistaken; and he remarked that 'for what regularities that do exist we owe far more to the printers than to the scholars'[10], though modern experts on the printing of the first editions of Shakespeare's plays would have something to say to that. With the development of commerce, industry and the sciences the language has been augmented with an abundance of words of foreign origin, and many 'professional' words have been created from Greek and Latin roots. It is now a rich mixture, used by many millions. Bodmer's name for it was 'Anglo-American', which would not have satisfied H. L. Mencken, who thought that, as used in the United States, so much of the language is indigenous and far more vital and expressive than the language of the British that he felt fully entitled to call his book on the subject *The AMERICAN Language*[11]. The book and its two supplements are a fund of information about the use of words, diligently compiled and entertainingly discussed; the work not of an expert in linguistics, as Mencken said himself, but of a journalist interested in language. He was content to describe, without criticism, the many transfusions into the language from immigrant sources, and local usages in American speech, state by state. He evidently felt free to express his opinions about *manner* in speech. He despised the 'affectations of the Hudson valley Anglomaniacs'; indeed, his dislike of the English (and not only for their way with the language) was intolerant in the extreme, and it diminished the value of his work, as A. J. Leibling pointed out.[12] But Mencken was justified in claiming autonomy for American pronunciation, spelling and idiom, and he was acknowledged as a valuable contributor to the authorative *Dictionary of Americanisms*, whose two large volumes contain thousands of words and expressions that have originated in the United States, most of them unknown on the other side of the Atlantic. They change and multiply, under the influence of computer-speak, rock-speak and much else. Leibling thought that the differences between American and English do not much matter; but in the opinion of Robert Burch-field, the distinguished former chief editor of the *Oxford English Dictionary*,[13] the languages of America and Britain are slowly but inexorably moving towards a state of mutual incomprehen-sion. It is evidently already happening. In 1965 a contributor to *Printing & Graphic Arts*, reviewing a book that had originated in London, noted reproachfully that 'the editing did not include a combing-over for briticisms, so that the message does not come through quite as clearly as it should for the American audience'.[14] (That lower-case *b* is mortifying!)

Mencken's assertion that 'American spelling is plainly better than English spelling'[15] is reasonable enough, the American way being more consistent in its spelling of words having elements in common: for instance, the -*or* ending, as in *color, governor, vapor*; the use of *s*, not *c*, in *defense* and *pretense* as well as *expense* and *recompense*; and so on. Americans are more willing than the British to coin new spellings, and put them to use. *Show-biz, tonite, burlesk*, and *foto* are only a few of many such forms contrived by that august journal *Variety*; its *whodunit*, a happy invention, entered British dictionaries years ago. In the 1930s the Chicago *Tribune*[16] set out a list of eighty-odd words it proposed to spell in its own way: for example, *burocracy, lether, sherif, trafic, warant*. In 1939 the paper abandoned most of them, but in 1946 it tried a few more: *thru, altho, geografy* were amongst them. The New York *Daily News*, under the influence of the *Tribune* (and perhaps of *Variety*) adopted a few of its spellings, including words where *f* could be substituted for *ph*, as in *tele-graf* and *foto*, though as Mencken pointed out, the paper went only half-way with *fotographer*. Changes of that sort are for space-saving reasons; they would not satisfy serious reformers, most of whom insist that all words should be represented *as heard*, phonetically, the sounds of the words being expressed in characters that have only one invariable phonetic value.

The spoken versions of the language involve a multiplicity of sounds which, if they were to be written and printed unam-biguously, would require letters or symbols for at least twenty distinct consonants and the same number of vowels and diph-thongs – though the experts differ as to numbers.[17] As it is, we represent the language with an alphabet developed originally for Latin, which had a very narrow range of vowel sounds, suffi-ciently served by the letters *a, e, i, o* and *u*. In addition to those we make *y* act as vowel as well as consonant, and *w* is joined to some vowels to produce diphthongs. Anomalies abound: *throw* and *now*, *dough* and *rough*, *move* and *love*, and many more. On the other hand, the visual difference between words of the same sound is a significant aid to meaning, as in *you* and *yew*, *horse* and *hoarse*, *piece* and *peace*, *flour* and *flower*. In our daily affairs most of us born to the language are concerned first with meaning, secondly with pronunciation, and hardly at all with the caprices of spelling and the frugality of the alphabet, taking them for granted. The advocates of reform regard that attitude as ineffi-cient, responsible for difficulties in the teaching of children and foreign students. (Incidentally, it is not only English spelling that is frequently eccentric; consider the sound represented by the six letters in *oiseau*). Some reformers have taken the view that the most practical way to achieve a revision of spelling is to retain the present alphabet, which typesetting machines are able to cope with, but to discard the letters *q* and *x* and either *c* or *k*, because they are redundant. Benn Pitman of 'Sinsinati' (his spelling) thought like that, though for a different reason. 'The eye of the average reader, once trained to appreciate the symmetry and beauty of the Roman forms, will not be satisfied with hybrid types ...'[18] by which he meant invented characters. He was on uncertain ground in assuming that the average reader has taste in letter forms, because that requires study and judgement. Another phonetician who proposed a scheme which used only the regular alphabet was Alexander Ellis. His reformed spelling looked like this (the emphasised syllable was to be followed by a point):

> Introadeu·s along·seid ov dhi oald speling a neu aurthog·rafi, konsisting ov dhi oald leters euzd invair·riabli in dhair best noan sensez.[19]

That mode required diphthongs to represent certain vowel sounds: for example, *oa* for long *o*, *eu* for long *u*. Isaac Pitman of Bath (elder brother of Benn) took a different course. He augmen-ted the common alphabet with an array of phonetic characters, some invented and others borrowed from Greek; had them made in type and used them in many publications from 1846 on-wards.[20] His object was to enable people, especially foreign stu-dents, to pronounce words correctly – that is, in the so-called 'proper' English of southern England – not to teach them to read

5. Hou tu Grʊ Wįz.

If lit-el boiz and gerlz wiʃ tu be-kʊm gud and wįz, ꝺɛ mʊst duɯ whot iz rįt, and lern sʊm-ꝺiŋ nɥ ev-er-i dɛ.

Isaac Pitman's fonetiks

existing literature. (The spelling reformer has to face the fact that even if his scheme should actually be adopted to help the child or foreigner to *speak* the language, traditional spelling will also have to be learnt as a second stage of education if the existing resources of the world's libraries are to continue in use).

Pitman's phonetic alphabet included special characters to represent the *th* and *ng* sounds that are so frequent in English. Legros and Grant selected those two digraphs for one of the

ĦE SAVIŊ EFFECTED BY REFORMIŊ ĦE ALPHABET.

Ħe one ħiŋ, above all ħiŋs, ħat seemiŋly is required in ħe printiŋ of newspapers, is ħe saviŋ of time in goiŋ to press.   In ħe second place, ħe saviŋ of time, and ħerefore ħe saviŋ of money in composiŋ, is of ħe greatest importance and ever-increasiŋ interest to ħe trade.   Ħirdly, ħe mere alteriŋ or addiŋ of a unit ensures a saviŋ in space well worħ ħe publisher giviŋ it serious attention.   Ħis saviŋ in ħe case of newspapers

Legros and Grant's digraphs

statistical studies they were keen on, and concluded that if just those two items were designed as single-character logotypes and adopted by the newspapers of Britain and America there would be a saving of about three-and-a-half per cent in column inches and composing time, which in monetary terms would mean a considerable sum. 'By dividing this saving between the operators and the proprietors, the aggregate sum gained by each of them yearly would in itself amount to a fortune'[21] – which shows a touching belief in the benevolence of newspaper proprietors.

The sound values given to the vowel letters and some consonants of the Roman alphabet vary from one country and language to another. During the nineteenth century, when linguistics was developed into a science, the phonologists formed the International Phonetic Association (1886) and drew up an international phonetic alphabet as a universal means of representing in print the fricatives, plosives, affricates, velars and other sounds that they detect in the speech of Eliza Doolittle and anyone else to whom they give ear. In Mergenthaler Linotype's list there were over two hundred IPA phonetic characters and symbols, all lower-case. A few of them are invented shapes, but most of them are familiar letters behaving in an unfamiliar way: upside down,

'wʌn 'nʌɪt ðə 'ræts 'hɜd eɪ 'greɪt 'nɔɪz
ɪn ðə 'lɑ̈ft| ɪt wəz ə 'vɛrɪ 'drɪrɪ oʊl
'lɑ̈ft| ðə 'ruf lɛr 'ɪn ðə 'reꞀɪn| ðə 'bimz
ˀæn 'rɑftəz wə 'ɔl 'rɑtn̩| so ðət ðə 'pleɪs
wəz 'rɑðə ʌn'seɪf| ət 'lɑst 'wʌn əv ðə
'dʒɔɪs 'geꞀɪv 'weꞀɪ| æn ðə 'bimz 'fɛl wɪð
'wʌn ˀɛnd ɒn ðə 'floʊʌ| ðə 'wɔl 'ʃuk|
ˀænd 'ɔl ðə 'ræts 'hɛə 'stʊd ɒn 'ɛnd| wɪθ

The IPA phonetic characters in action

back to front, or wearing tails or marks of various kinds. Incomprehensible to the layman, they are a tool for the specialist who records in print the nuances of speech habits. People who produce dictionaries usually limit the use of phonetic characters to the few that the ordinary reader can be expected to learn.

As a branch of linguistic science phonetics is technical and complicated, and it is doubtful wisdom for graphic designers who are not expert linguists to venture into that field and publish proposals for phonetic alphabets to be used by the general public. The fact that Jan Tschichold did so is an example of the enthusiasm for reform that was current in German artistic circles in the 1920s. Herbert Bayer, too, after his move to America in 1938, proposed a reformed alphabet that included a number of phonetic characters: some to stand for single sounds traditionally represented as *ch*, *th* and *sh*; others to indicate *ion* and *ng*.[22] His scheme also included ideas for spelling reform: *f* in place of *ph*, thus *frase* and *alfabet* (Bayer had settled in Chicago, and may have noticed the spelling habits of the *Tribune*); *k* and *s* for hard and soft *c* – though in his illustrations the word 'condition' retains the initial *c*. He suggested three forms of the vowel *o*, but seemed to think that the vowel sounds in *of* and *other* are the same. In the illustrated word *efektiv* only one form of *e* is used for two very different sounds. Not that these errors are important: the scheme was an outline, not a finished proposal. But they do show that phonetics and spelling reform are areas to be entered (if at all) with considerable caution. Robert Bridges, the English poet who spent a great deal of time and thought in devising a system of phonotypes, is quoted as saying about the 'tyranny of our spelling system' that those who uphold it 'are playing into the hands of the revolutionists ... who would substitute the worse tyranny of a questionable phonetic system'.[23] H. W. Fowler thought that spelling reform, like war, was too serious a subject to be left to the experts: '... most reformers are so much more awake to the obvious advantages of change than to its less obvious evils that we cannot trust them with the disposal of so vastly important a matter'.[24] In his view, little by little was the only feasible way.

Bayer's zeal for changing the appearance of the printed word had been developed during his time at the Bauhaus. He was one of the 'fluent Teutons' whose ideas disturbed Stanley Morison, and not only because, along with others, he asserted that only the sans-serif letter was true to the spirit of the time. It must have been Morison who had spoken to Updike of his disapproval of the theory that capitals are unnecessary: lower case is all we need.[25] The theory had been advanced in Germany by a Dr Porstmann in 1920 and supported (for what it was worth) by the association of engineers there.[26] It may have had some attraction for those who disliked the visual effect of the custom of capitalis-

ing the first letter in every German noun. One of the advocates of
the theory was Herbert Bayer who, by his own account, proposed in 1925 that the printing at the Bauhaus should be done
without capitals. (Actually, the prohibition was on the use of
capitals as initials to words in lower case, including the first word
in a sentence. The capital alphabet in its own right continued to
be used in display work). Bayer offered several reasons. 'Writing-
printing only with lower case saves time' (not so: the same number of letters are needed whatever their shape); 'saves money' (for
the printer in his outlay on equipment, perhaps, but not for his
customer); 'makes reading easier' (the text matter of his own
book, set entirely without capitals even for personal names,
hardly supports the claim).[27] His logic was shaky, but some of
the original attraction of the theory may have been in its value as
a revolutionary gesture. The idea appears to have affronted
Morison's belief that typography must be familiar and according
to custom. Updike told him there was nothing to be excited
about; the idea had turned up more than once in the past and had
had no serious effect whatever. In fact, there was an example
fairly close to Morison's hand. In Thibaudeau's *Manuel de
Typographie Moderne** there was an account of the style of
typographic treatment favoured by the designer Coquemer for
artistic stationery and advertising. A particular feature of it was
the total absence of capitals. Thibaudeau thought that that, and
the designer's use of a single typeface, the Nicholas Cochin, was
a charming fashion, a way of achieving *'du grand chic'*.[28] If

les acacias

j a r d i n - r e s t a u r a n t

47, rue des acacias (étoile)
téléphone : wagram 37-66 et 91-70

besson, propriétaire

Typography by Coquemer,
from Thibaudeau's *Manuel de
Typographie Moderne*,
Paris, 1924

Morison had noticed that it might have persuaded him that the
idea need not be taken seriously, on the ground that if working
typographers took any notice of it at all they would disregard the
theory and simply use the notion as an agreeable but ephemeral
trick of display. But the theory continued to irk Morison; he
referred to it, and to Bayer, with what reads like reluctant re-
straint at the end of his *Politics and Script*,[29] which was published
posthumously. Bayer's own book on his career is typeset in the
lower-case-only mode, which means that the first person singular

* Morison knew of the work. He included it in the bibliography at the end of his
article on typography on page 652 of the *Encyclopedia Britannica*, 1929 edition.

pronoun is a lower-case *i* – as it was, incidentally, in the preface to the first volume of Ames and Herbert's *Typographical Antiquities* (1785).[30] The effect is slightly comical, bringing to mind Archy's typewritten letters about Mehitabel, where the humour is visual as well as verbal. Some such thought may have occurred

```
see here mehitabel
i said i thought
you told me that
it was cleopatra
you used to be
before you
transmigrated into
the carcase of a cat
where do you get
this tut
ankh
amen stuff
question mark
```

From *archy and mehitabel* by Don Marquis, 1927

Archy, once a poet, now a cockroach, used the office typewriter after hours, but could not manage the shift key.

to Bayer. In his foreword to Arthur A. Cohen's survey of his work the pronoun is *I* – the only capital in the book.[31] As a display device the lower-case-only idea shows up sometimes on shop fascias; and a London publishing house recently started to signify itself (not very loudly) as **ff**. Sometimes necessity rules. On London's underground railway stations the electronic indicators, which use dot-matrix characters, cannot offer capitals and lower case in the same line, so travellers have learnt to recognise 'charing cross' and 'camden town'.

The lower-case-only mode has never had serious support, even amongst admirers of the Bauhaus ethos, or those who think it a hardship for children to have to learn two shapes for each letter. 'Are capitals necessary?' is a non-question. Their practical value is undeniable, and far outweighs any illogicality there may be in their existence. In this kind of matter logic is an over-rated commodity.

The alphabet itself has been criticised. No time need be given to Eric Gill's assertion that writing, and therefore the printed word, is 'an entirely outworn, decayed and corrupt convention'[32] and that letters should be replaced by shorthand symbols: he was simply being provocative. And George Bernard Shaw was amusing himself when he wrote into his will a legacy to pay for the invention of an entirely new alphabet. Others have taken the alphabet seriously, but disapproved of some aspects of it. There was the belief that the English language in print would acquire some of the pleasing smoothness of Latin if the ascending parts of b, d, f, h, k and l were shortened and the letters, g, j, p, q and y were reshaped to eliminate the descending parts altogether. In

1804 Philip Rusher of Banbury published an edition of Samuel Johnson's *Rasselas* printed with such 'improved' characters. 'More curious than beautiful' was Reed's verdict.[33] Over a century later the idea was referred to approvingly in a pamphlet by the Dean of Derry in northern Ireland.[34] W. A. Dwiggins, the eminent American type designer, knew the pamphlet, took notice of its theme that Latin is visually more attractive than English, and in the 1940s he proposed, with some seriousness, that text matter would look better if certain lower-case letters* were used in uncial form rather than the familiar shape.

Those proposals had an aesthetic motive. There were others of functional intent. Legros and Grant accused some roman lower-case letters of resembling others.[35] They thought e could be confused with o or c, n with u, i with l, h with b, and a with s. They set up an elaborate study in which enlarged letters were superimposed and their common and distinctive areas carefully measured and tabulated as illegibility and legibility co-efficients. They found that in an old-style face the 'similar' letters were more easily recognised than in a modern face, and that the Blackfriars

Recent Years

The Blackfriars type

type (modestly described as 'produced under the direction of one of the authors') performed better than either.

Herbert Bayer followed a similar track. 'If the individual letters are similar to each other and by their design harmony contain little contrast, perception will be slow.'[36] It certainly sometimes occurs that in a sans-serif type (the form he preferred), when set in a small size and badly printed, the i, l and I may resemble each other. In a seriffed type that seldom happens; the serifs help to differentiate the letters. 'Reading should become less of an effort when each letter is designed clearly and more distinctively from all others'; and in support of that opinion Bayer offered his 'basic alfabet'. These are some of its characters:

pmsnʌoɛдɕ

Bayer was taking a strictly utilitarian view of letter forms, and presumably would not have admitted an aesthetic comment into any discussion of those 'clearer' shapes, on the ground that we are so thoroughly conditioned by the familiar existing forms that we cannot detach ourselves sufficiently to make an objective judgement.

The re-structuring of traditional letter forms was also sug-

* They are shown on page 191 of the author's *Letters of Credit: a view of type design* (1986).

gested in a research study published in 1969[37]. For test purposes some Harvard and MIT men were presented with pages of words and letter groups arranged normally, upside down, reversed right to left and in combinations of those settings, and their rate of reading was recorded. From the results the researcher formed the opinion that it is the right-hand side of a letter which provides us with the clue to its identity. He had been told that a letter designer 'makes his downstrokes heavy and his upstrokes and curves light', which sounds like a garbled reference to calligraphic work or to types in which the strokes are of different thicknesses. But he employed a sans-serif face to support the theory, a standard design used by the U.S. Bureau of Public Roads: not a good choice, because its capitals are wide and its lower case narrow. When halved vertically, the left and right sides of most of the lower case characters were equally obscure. However, the researcher was satisfied, and arranged for capital and lower-case alphabets to be specially drawn with the right-hand side of the letters emphasised, the left side having few heavy lines. The outcome was prudently offered 'not as prescription

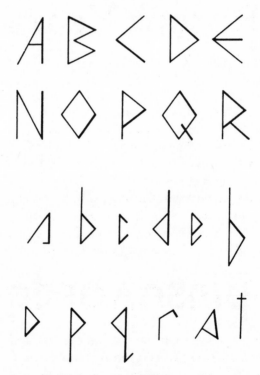

Some of the tentative letter forms by Jerome Abelman for the Kolers study

but as illustration'. 'In constructing it we have tried to stay within the conventions that define the letters of the Roman alphabet, but there is no reason in principle that these ancient marks cannot be changed.' (The air of confidence in that last statement is reminiscent of Frederick Bodmer's admiring reference to Kemal Ataturk's direction to the Turks to adopt the

Roman alphabet[38]: 'Some people say that we cannot change people's language habits by Act of Parliament' – thus showing a blithe disregard for the difference between the processes of democracy and of despotism, however benevolent.)

The fundamental error in that project, as in Legros and Grant's study of resemblances, is the assumption that a reader has to recognise *each letter* before he can recognise each word. But it has been shown, and experience confirms it, that the competent reader's eyes take in a text not by nibbling at it unit by unit but by gulping groups of words; and – such is the speed at which the perceptive faculty operates – even failing to notice a wrong letter in a word.

Psychologists, and engineers like Lucien Legros, need to *measure* things: cognition, parts of letters, anything that can be identified and then evaluated by time or dimension. They make up a theory, devise a testing procedure, tabulate the results, and draw a conclusion. What they do not include in their studies of the reading process is the effect that the text has on the mind of the individual reader. It is not included because it is not measurable in any sense that can be embodied in a generalisation. But simply to measure comprehension is not enough: that does little more than show that the 'guinea pigs' engaged in the project can read and that the test material is intelligible. In real life the effect of a text on the sentient mind is central and irremovable from the reading process. The mental pleasure that a good novel gives us, and the drift of its narrative, actually help us to anticipate the words to come; comprehension is swift and eager. By contrast, the text of a state enactment or a judicial report, say, may be hard going. To put it in typographic terms: a novel set in eleven point Sabon two point leaded with an average of eleven words to the line may well be easy and stimulating to read; but offer it to another person and it will be rejected because he or she dislikes the author's work. A legal text book set in precisely the same way (should the publisher have the good taste to see to it) may yet have the reader stumbling through unfamiliar ideas and phrases and not at all certain of his comprehension of the work. In reality, willingness and effort are aspects of reading that make it more than a measurable process; it is an *experience*, compounded of purpose, mood, time, pleasure or duty – human responses so variable that the researcher is compelled to deny their existence as the only way of reducing his project to manageable form.

'Typographers and other graphic designers have continued to hold research at arm's length, with an odd mixture of awe and distrust.'[39] The comment echoes the one quoted earlier; different words but the same hint of reproach. The implication is that typographers should, but don't, take some sort of active role in research, initiating projects themselves or at least encouraging others. The fact is, though, that so far from being suspicious of research, typographers are mostly indifferent to it. And with reason. Naturally, typographers admire the efforts of those who explore ways and means of helping children and the handicapped to read; and, too, they can see the case for research into specific matters like the legibility of directory entries, the details in military maps, the layout of official questionnaires, the organising of tabulations in a viewdata system, the design of alphabets for low-resolution print-out devices, and other particular tasks. But the majority of typographers are engaged in commercial work of some sort, the putting together of words and pictures in a form that will attract and hold the attention of a fickle public. At the mention of research they may look around at the typographic scene and observe the millions of 'visible words' that are produced every day in the form of newspapers, books, magazines, mailing shots and professional material of every sort. They know that the common element in it all is the familiar alphabet. They do not hear expressions of dismay from publishers and advertisers that their printed material is being rejected because the public is baffled by the spelling or the shapes of the letters; on the contrary, in practice all this visible language works very well. (The fact that much of the daily yield of print is not actually read is due to the readers' habits of selection, not to the print being incomprehensible.) If a particular item fails in its purpose the fault lies not in the language or the alphabet but in the way the matter is presented: in short, in incompetent typography.

The typographers may then look more closely at the research projects about which they are said to be neglectful. Some deal with aspects of illiteracy – matter for the educationist, not the designer, unless he is invited to take part. A few projects deal with a particular area of typographic design: scientific text books, say; important for typographers in that field but of limited interest to those whose professional concern is with a fashion magazine or the design of package holiday brochures. A great deal of the research, though, seems to be produced by academics for the interest not of designers but of other academics. Their motives are easy to understand: there is the need to add another title to their list of publications, that being the way to academic advancement. And there is the attraction of begetting a new item of knowledge for its own sake, regardless of its practical value, or lack of it. Typographic designers see no reason for guilt at ignoring academic research projects that treat an aspect of legibility or readability as a case for statistical analysis and which use for laboratory purposes a group of 'subjects' who seldom accord with the typographers' idea of the typical reader.

The designers then look to themselves. If they are sufficiently realistic and detached they recognise that they are simply the ones in the middle, helping A to gain the attention of C. They take a utilitarian view of things. They cannot tell their clients that they should adopt simplified spelling, and they cannot themselves insist on using phonetic characters or a reformed alphabet. The most they can do with the words and pictures they have been given is to arrange them with sense and taste; and if publicity work is their métier, to freshen up the motifs of display typography. For them, research and reform are occasionally interesting, frequently bewildering, but rarely of any consequence in the typographic scene as they know it.

Coda

In the 1960s, when it became clear that metal typesetting and letterpress printing were giving way to electronic typesetting and offset lithography, there were two quite different views of the effect that the new technology would have on the design of type faces and the ideas of the typographer. In the offices of the typesetting machine manufacturers the engineers and their colleagues in charge of typeface production had no thought of altering the appearance of print. On the contrary, they knew that publishers and printers would only take an interest in the new technology, however remarkable its output rate, if it would provide typesetting identical in appearance with what they and the reading public were used to. By contrast, the typographers – that is, those who wrote about typography – looked at the prospect with wide-eyed speculation and prophesied extraordinary changes in the appearance of print. For example: 'The rapid extension of automation and the application of electronics involves a radically changed outlook upon all past and present habits of thought and systems of production. These changes in technique . . . carry with them changes also in outlook upon design . . .'[1] And from another source: 'During the next quarter of a century the visible word will change dramatically under the impact of electronics . . . The norm in lettering today is the printed letter; tomorrow it will be the photo-electric letter.'[2] And from a different quarter: 'Phototype, being unrestricted by the conditions governing the production and use of metal type will, in time, alter its design characteristics.'[3] This was rather like believing that a change from gas cooking to electric would lead to the creation of extraordinary new dishes.

The idea that typographic letter forms may be influenced by the way they are made is entirely fallacious. The methods of producing metal type imposed few restrictions of any consequence on the design of type faces, as a glance at the scripts and novelties of the past makes clear. The methods of producing type for electronic typesetting systems and of outputting it on to film are certainly quite different from those that applied to metal type; but in both cases the methods are simply different means to the same end, letters in print. If the design characteristics of letters are to be changed in any radical way in the future it will not be due to a special feature of the production method but to a request from the market place, as was the case, for instance, when the E-13B bank cheque characters and, in another field, the Initial Teaching Alphabet were instigated.

The predicted 'photo-electric letter' – meaning, presumably, one that is distinctly different from the traditional form because of its electronic genesis – is actually only to be seen in the output of print-out devices attached to computers, the awkward shape of the letter being due to the limitations of the system: tolerated for functional reasons but necessarily short on aesthetic quality. In the appearance of print itself the effect of electronic typesetting has been minimal. It has certainly facilitated the creation of new type faces; but apart from a few 'novelty' display types all of

A dot-matrix print-out

```
        MERMAID  THEATRE
Barbican  PUDDLE DOCK, BLACKFRIARS
BBCentre  LONDON EC4V  3DB

        The RSC at THE MERMAID in
        THEY SHOOT HORSES

        £8.50
        SAT 11 JUL 87  7:30 PM
        STALLS      RIGHT P17
```

them have been designed in one or other of the styles developed long ago and could, in fact, have been made as easily in metal as by photographic or digital means. It could not have been otherwise. The act and habit of reading, and the printed matter we use for it, are a continuum, extending from person to person and back and forth in time. For example, an article in today's newspaper, quoting a parliamentary report of some years ago, may itself be consulted by a future historian. It is unrealistic to assume that people will willingly consent to read unusual letter forms presented in unfamiliar arrangements just because the producers have adopted a new system of production. The *amount* of print may increase because of new production methods; the *nature* of it, familiar alphabet characters forming comprehensible words arranged in lineal sequence, is immutable.

Such changes that have occurred in the appearance of print in the past quarter-century have been due not to electronic typesetting but to the method of printing itself, the process of depositing words and pictures on paper: that is, to offset-litho technology which, with its highly-developed combination of photographic and chemical transfers and sophisticated electronic control systems, has relegated the traditional letterpress process to the field of the 'private' printer. It is the picture, coloured or black-and-white, that has benefitted most from the improved quality of reproduction; and designers are influenced by that fact. In some magazines now the pictures are so prominent that the text seems to be there simply to separate the pictures. 'The picture aggressing on the prose,' as Stanley Morison remarked about popular tabloid newspapers.[4] Newspapers themselves, or at least the best of them, are now so much better because they are offset-printed that their photographs are clear enough to confirm that the captions are fact, not fiction. On the whole, though, books have not been enhanced by the offset-litho process, which tends to be unsympathetic to type. In the ordinary paperback, the staple of the airport news stand, the text type is sometimes as degraded as it was in the pulp magazines of the thirties. In the hardback book, even when it is not illustrated, the paper is often of a disagreeable whiteness, on which the type, its serifs frequently eroded, stares at the reader. 'The avoidance of bleak white papers by our better-informed printers has been a decided step in the right direction.'[5] Bruce Rogers said that in 1943. He would not have been pleased with the condition of books today.

Print on paper is not the only vehicle of verbal communication. Large numbers of people, including children, now spend time absorbing information from the screen of the visual display unit of a personal computer. The characters they watch are simple representations of our familiar letters and numerals, a sub-species of the sans-serif; individually more or less legible, recognisable when grouped in words as a context, sufficient for their purpose. To call them crude is unfair. Their 'primitive' shapes are due to two limiting factors: they are formed of bits of light, each bit an electronic signal from a computer's memory store; and that memory, though capacious, is needed for many functions, so the screen letter forms are made as economically as possible. Aesthetic criteria cannot be applied severely; but though none of them are attractive, many are worse than they need be.

There is another area of visual communication where screen letter forms can certainly be judged in aesthetic terms: the graphics of television commercials and program introductions. For years they were informative but seldom visually interesting, their origins all too obviously dry-transfer or simple photo-set lettering on a series of boards, with sometimes the traditional devices of the movie technician, the fade, the wipe and so on, to enliven the sequence. Electronics and the computer have now provided the means for new and stimulating effects, and movement, colour and sound are often combined with great ingenuity to imprint the message or title on the viewers' retinas and, it is hoped, on their minds. The sophisticated equipment now employed by television companies enables them to use letter forms in considerable variety, and even, very sensibly, to commission new faces for their exclusive use. Such faces can be called typographic, in that though they are original and distinctive they exhibit the characteristics of letter forms developed in the past for printed work.

The visual introduction to a regular television programme is often now an enjoyable experience in itself, and praiseworthy evidence that a designer has matched his imagination and inventiveness to the technical resources available to him. But its repetition over a long period means that the enjoyment is of a diminishing order, replaced quite soon by indifference and then boredom. Magazine publishers, even of serious journals, discovered long ago that to repeat the same front cover issue after issue was a practice of negative value. They saw that though the title piece, the journal's 'signature', should be unchanged as evidence of continuity, the front of each number had better exhibit something fresh to persuade the reader that the journal was not just the mixture as before. If television programme producers would invite their graphics people to vary the form of a programme's introduction, within a recognisable formula, they might increase their chances of keeping the viewers' affection and their place in those curious measures of merit, the ratings.

The visible word, then, is not just the printed word. Indeed, it never was: think of the multitude of street signs and shop fascias we see every day. But it is words on paper, print in all its variety, that constitute the typographic scene. However, the development of the computer and the possibilities of storage and retrieval with the aid of a visual display screen raised the question as to whether or not the printed word had a future. In 1980 a number of specialists were asked for their views. One of them, referring to a particular area of communication, wrote: 'The predominant mechanism for transfer of scientific and technical information will continue to be print on paper. The creators of primary information will resist, and successfully, any attempt to replace the convenience and ego-enhancing qualities of the printed page in the conventional scientific journal by any presently foreseeable substitute.'[6] And another, in more general terms: '. . . a point that the enthusiast for electronic communication and new media all too often overlooks: no matter how the information is transmitted and displayed, no matter what kinds of exotic technology we employ, people will *still be reading*'.[7] (That word 'information', by the way, is used by specialists as a single hold-all term for things printed – but only because a better term is difficult to find. It looks odd as a description of the work of a poet or novelist, but it serves quite well for works of reference, like a thesaurus or the Michelin guide, for technical and scientific text books, and for much of the work produced in desktop publishing.) Databanks and the print-outs that are extracted from them have grown apace since those views were recorded. But although the terminal and the television screen now occupy much of the leisure time of many people, words in print continue to appear. Indeed, they proliferate – and not simply as secondary companions to pictures.

If the words fail to get all the attention their authors hope for, it may be because our response to any piece of print – from keen interest to indifference and rejection – often depends on how well the typographer has presented the words to us; and that depends on his attitude to the task. It should not be difficult for him to adopt one if the maxim of that great designer Eileen Gray is constantly in mind; 'To create, one must first question everything.'[8] After all, the typographer is himself sometimes a reader; and like a professional cook visiting a restaurant for a meal, he is (or should be) critical of what is produced by others, and equally analytical about his own work.

References

Advent

1   Henry Stevens, *Who spoils our English Books?* (London, 1884)
2   Walter Gillis, 'Caslon Old Style Type', *The Graphic Arts*, vol. I (Boston, 1911), pp.128–36
3   Carl Purington Rollins, 'Whither Now, Typographer?': an address to the Society of Printers, Boston, 1936. Printed in *Off the Dead Bank*, The Typophiles (New York, 1949), pp.54
4   Will Bradley, *Notes towards an Autobiography* (New York, 1955); included in *Will Bradley, his Graphic Art*, edited by Clarence P. Hornung (New York, 1974)
5   A. J. A. Symons, 'An Unacknowledged Movement in Fine Printing', *The Fleuron*, VII, p.107
6   Bruce Rogers, 'An Address', *The Work of Bruce Rogers* (New York, 1939), p.xli
7   Clarence P. Hornung, *Will Bradley, his Graphic Art* (New York, 1974), plates 27, 53
8   American Type Founders Company, *The American Chap-Book*, twelve numbers (Jersey City, Sept 1904 to August 1905)
9   Sir Francis Meynell, *My Lives* (London, 1971), p.135

The march of type

1   T. L. De Vinne, *The Practice of Typography: Plain Printing Types* (New York, 1900), pp.376–7
2   J. L. Frazier, *Type Lore* (Chicago, 1925)
3   D. B. Updike, *Printing Types, their History, Form and Use*, vol. II, second edition (Cambridge, Mass. 1937), p.235
4   Douglas C. McMurtrie, *American Type Design in the Twentieth Century* (Chicago, 1924), p.30
5   Paul Beaujon [Beatrice Warde], 'The "Garamond" Types: sixteenth and seventeenth century sources considered', *The Fleuron*, V (London, 1926), p.176
6   John Dreyfus, 'The Baskerville Punches, 1750–1950', *The Library* (London, June 1950), p.46
7   McMurtrie, *American Type Design*, p.30
8   Stanley Morison, *Printing The Times since 1785* (London, 1953), p.165
9   A. F. Johnson, *Type Designs, their History and Development*, second edition (London, 1959), p.132
10 Stanley Morison, 'On Script Types', *The Fleuron*, IV (London, 1925), p.39
11 Updike, *Printing Types*, vol. II, p.291
12 R. S. Hutchings, 'Post-war Type Design in Germany', *British Printer* (May 1962), pp.145–52
13 Harry Carter, 'Collins Fontana Type', *Signature*, 4 (November 1936), pp.42–6

Mentors

1   T. L. De Vinne, *The Practice of Typography: a treatise on the processes of type-making, etc.* (New York, 1900); *Correct Composition* (1901); *A Treatise on Title Pages* (1902); *Modern Methods of Book Composition* (1904)
2   John Southward, 'Art in Book Printing: a study of the Aesthetics of Typography' (lecture), *British and Colonial Printer* (London, 6 February 1896), pp.65–6
3   T. L. De Vinne, 'Masculine Printing', *United Typothetae of America, 6th Convention* (1892), pp.163–73
4   Carl Purington Rollins, *Theodore Low De Vinne*, The Typophiles (New York, 1968), vol. I, p.24
5   T. L. De Vinne, *Historic Printing Types*, lecture at The Grolier Club, January 1885 (New York, 1886)
6   Talbot Baines Reed, 'Old and New Fashions in Typography', lecture at the Society of Arts, April 1890, in *Caslon's Circular* (Summer 1890)
7   Harry Carter, *Typography*, 5 (London, 1938), p.28

8 A. F. Johnson, *Type Designs, their History and Development*, second edition (London, 1959)

9 Stanley Morison, *A Tally of Types, with additions by several hands*, edited by Brooke Crutchley (Cambridge, 1973)

10 *The Fleuron*, No. VII, edited by Stanley Morison (Cambridge, 1930), pp.61–72

11 *Ibid*, p.250

12 Eric Gill, *An Essay on Typography* (1931); revised edition (London, 1936; re-set 1954), p.70

13 *Paragraphs on Printing, elicited from Bruce Rogers in talks with James Hendrickson* (New York, 1943; reprinted 1979), p.57

14 Stanley Morison, *The 2 kinds of Effectiveness*, leaflet written for the conference of the Master Printers' Federation (Blackpool, 1928)

15 Stanley Morison, 'On Advertisement Settings', *Signature*, 3 (London, July 1936), pp.1–6

16 *The Times Literary Supplement* (15 August 1936)

17 Holbrook Jackson, *The Printing of Books* (London, 1938), p.142

18 *Signature*, 5 (London, March 1937), pp.49–52

19 'Pierre Simon Fournier and XVIIIth century French Typography', in *The Monotype Recorder* (London, March–June 1926)

20 Paul Beaujon [Beatrice Warde], 'The "Garamond" Types: a study of XVI and XVII century sources', *The Fleuron*, V (Cambridge, 1926), pp.131–79

21 *The Monotype Recorder*, vol. 39, No. 4 (summer 1952), p.26

22 Beatrice Warde, 'Type Faces, Old and New', *The Library* (London, September 1935), pp.121–43

23 Carl Purington Rollins, 'Whither Now, Typographer?' *Off the Dead Bank*, The Typophiles (New York, 1949), pp.66–7

24 John Dreyfus, 'Beatrice Warde, First Lady of Typography', *Penrose Annual*, 63 (London, 1970), pp.69–76

25 Joseph Blumenthal, *The Spiral Press through Four Decades* (New York, 1966), p.38

26 *Stanley Morison and D. B. Updike: Selected Correspondence*, edited by David McKitterick (London, 1980), p.182

27 L. Moholy-Nagy, 'Die neue Typographie', *Staatliches Bauhaus in Weimar, 1919–23* (Munich, 1923); English translation in *Moholy-Nagy*, edited by Richard Kostelanetz (New York, 1970), pp.75–6

28 Herbert Spencer, *Pioneers of Modern Typography*, second edition (London, 1982)

29 W. A. Dwiggins, *Layout in Advertising* (New York, 1928), p.55

30 Stanley Morison, 'The Art of Printing', *Proceedings of the British Academy* (London, 1937), p.30

31 Stanley Morison to Robert Blake, May 1936; quoted in Nicolas Barker, *Stanley Morison* (London, 1972), p.350

32 In a talk recorded for the Double Crown Club, 1964

33 *Signature*, 3 (July 1936), pp.51–2

34 *Typography*, 2 (Spring 1937), p.22

35 Jan Tschichold, *Asymmetric Typography* (London and Toronto, 1967), p.20

36 Herbert Spencer, *Pioneers*, p.59

The typographic task

1 Jan Tschichold, *Asymmetric Typography* (London and Toronto, 1967), p.58

2 Hans Peter Willberg, 'Marginalia on remarks by Jan Tschichold', translated by Ruari McLean, in *Jan Tschichold, Typographer and Type Designer, 1902–1974*, catalogue of exhibition (Edinburgh, 1982), p.31

3 John Miles, *Design for Desktop Publishing* (London, 1987)

4 Ruari McLean, *Manual of Typography* (London, 1980)

Design: conservative and radical

1 *Books for our Time* (New York, 1951), the preamble

2 Jan Tschichold, *Asymmetric Typography*, p.19

3 Saul Bass, 'Thoughts on Design', an address at the Royal Society of Arts, May 1965; in *Royal Designers on Design* (London, 1986), p.116
4 Allen Hutt, *The Changing Newspaper* (London, 1973), p.88
5 *Ibid*, p.96
6 Jan Tschichold, *Eine Stunde Druckgestaltung* (Stuttgart, 1930), pp.77, 78
7 Hutt, *The Changing Newspaper*, p.107
8 *Linotype Matrix*, 16 (London, 1953), p.5

Reading: research: reform

1 James E. Allen, US Commissioner of Education, 'The right to read: target for the 70s', *Elementary English* (1970); reprinted in *Reading, Today and Tomorrow* (London, 1972), p.441
2 *The Independent*, (13 May 1987), p.1
3 Donald Moyle, 'Reading for the 70s', *Remedial Education* (1971). Reprinted in *Reading, Today and Tomorrow*, p.432
4 Edmund Fry, *Pantographia* (London, 1799), p.ii
5 Herbert Spencer, *The Visible Word* (London, 1969), bibliography
6 Jeremy J. Foster, *Legibility Research 1972–78* (London, 1980)
7 Paul A. Kolers, 'Clues to a Letter's Recognition', *The Journal of Typographic Research* (Cleveland, April 1969), p.146
8 Foster, *Legibility Research 1972–78*, p.77
9 Spencer, *The Visible Word*, p.6
10 Frederick Bodmer, *The Loom of Language* (London, 1944), p.83
11 H. L. Mencken, *The American Language*, Supplement II (New York, 1948), p.187
12 A. J. Leibling, ' The Tongue is Transatlantic', in the Book Week section of the *Sunday Herald Tribune* (New York, 24 November 1963)
13 A lecture in Chicago, 1978; mentioned in article by Robert McCrum, *The Times* (London, 18 September 1986)
14 *Printing and Graphic Arts*, vol. X, no. 2 (Lunenberg, Vermont, 1965), p.52
15 Mencken, *The American Language*, Supplement II, p.277
16 *Ibid*, pp.294–5
17 Bodmer, *The Loom of Language*, p.63
18 B. Pitman, 'The Scientific Representation of English from the Printer's Standpoint', *British & Colonial Printer* (April 1903), pp. 301–2
19 Alexander Ellis, 'On a practical Method of meeting the Spelling Difficulty in School and Life', paper read at the Society of Arts, 20 April 1870; in *Journal of the Society of Arts* (London, 1870)
20 I. Pitman, *The Sekond Buk of Fonetik Ridin* (London, 1876)
21 A. L. Legros, and J. C. Grant, *Typographical Printing Surfaces* (London, 1916), p.154
22 Herbert Bayer, 'basic alphabet', *Print* (May–June 1964), pp.16–19
23 Quoted in *Fowler's Modern English Usage*, second edition, revised by Sir Ernest Gowers (Oxford, 1965), p.575
24 H. W. Fowler, *Modern English Usage* (Oxford, 1944), p. 554
25 D. B. Updike, 'Some Tendencies in Modern Typography', extract from *Some Aspects of Printing Old and New* (1941), included in *Books and Printing*, pp. 306–12
26 L. Moholy-Nagy, 'Bauhaus and Typography'; English translation in H. M. Wingler, *The Bauhaus* (Cambridge, Mass. 1969), pp.114–15, and in *Moholy-Nagy*, edited by R. Kostelanetz (New York, 1970), pp.76–7
27 Herbert Bayer, 'basic alphabet', p.17
28 F. Thibaudeau, *Manuel de Typographie Moderne* (Paris, 1924), pp.247
29 Stanley Morison, *Politics and Script* (Oxford, 1972), p.337
30 Herbert Bayer, *herbert bayer, painter, designer, architect* (New York, 1967)
31 Arthur A. Cohen, *herbert bayer: the complete work* (Cambridge, Mass., 1984)
32 Eric Gill, *An Essay on Typography* (1931); revised edition (London, 1936; re-set 1954), p.117
33 T. B. Reed, *A History of Old English Letter Foundries*: new edition revised by A. F. Johnson (London, 1952), p.111

34 R. G. S. King, *Reflections on Printing Type Forms with Suggestions for Improvement* (Londonderry, 1926)

35 Legros and Grant, *Typographical Printing Surfaces*, p.160

36 Bayer, *herbert bayer, painter, designer, architect*, p.78

37 Kolers, *Journal of Typographic Research* (April 1969), p.164

38 Bodmer, *Loom of Language*, p.415

39 Merald E. Wrolstad, 'Letterform Research Needs Definition and Direction', *Journal of Typographic Research* (April 1969), p.119

Coda

1 Stanley Morison, Postscript to *First Principles* (1967)

2 Herbert Spencer, *The Visible Word*, p.9

3 Ben Rosen, *Type and Typography*, revised edition (New York, 1976), p.389

4 Stanley Morison, 'Picture printing and word printing', *Penrose Annual* (1956), p.25

5 Bruce Rogers, *Paragraphs on Printing* (New York, 1943; reprinted 1979), p.40

6 A. K. Kent, 'Scientific and Technical Publishing in the 1980s', *The Future of the Printed Word* (Milton Keynes, 1981), p.167

7 John M. Strawhorn, 'Future Methods and Techniques', *The Future of the Printed Word*, p.24

8 Peter Adam, *Eileen Gray, Architect/Designer* (New York, London, 1987). p.6

Index
An *italic* figure indicates an illustration